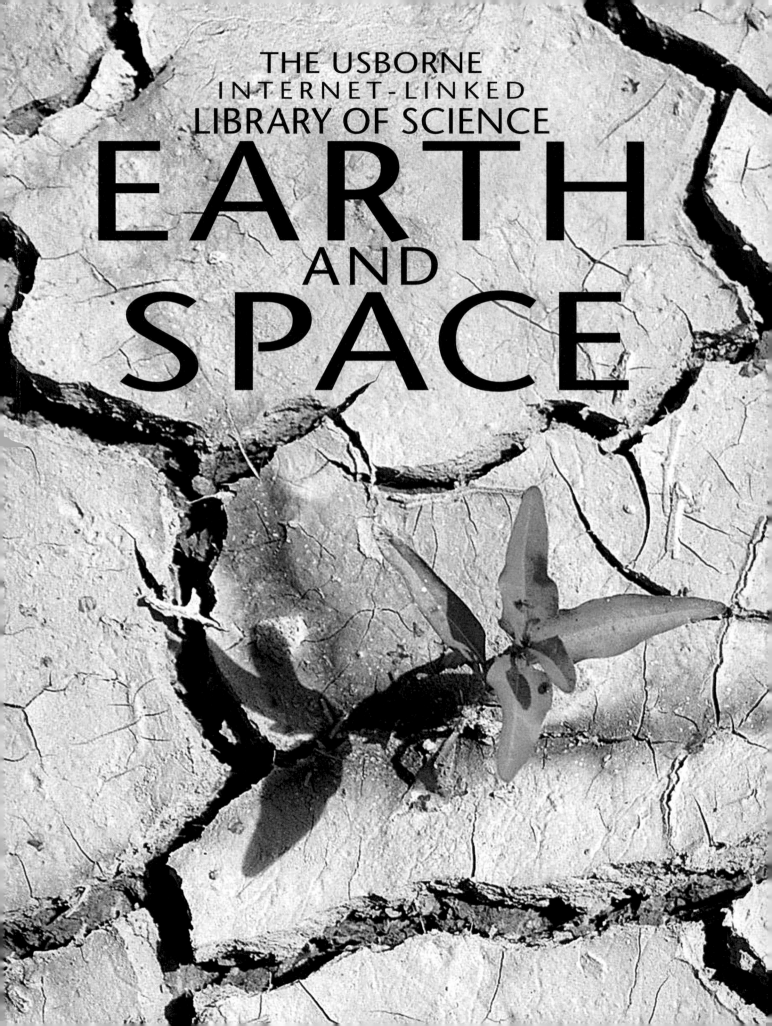

THE USBORNE
INTERNET-LINKED
LIBRARY OF SCIENCE

EARTH
AND
SPACE

First published in 2001 by Usborne Publishing Ltd,
Usborne House, 83-85 Saffron Hill, London EC1N 8RT, England.

www.usborne.com

Printed in Spain

AE First published in America, 2002.

THE USBORNE
INTERNET-LINKED
LIBRARY OF SCIENCE

EARTH
AND
SPACE

Laura Howell, Kirsteen Rogers
and Corinne Henderson

Designed by Ruth Russell, Chloë Rafferty,
Candice Whatmore, Karen Tomlins
and Adam Constantine

Digital illustrations by Verinder Bhachu
Digital imagery by Joanne Kirkby

Edited by Laura Howell

Cover design: Andrea Slane and Cristina Adami

Consultants: Dr Roger Trend and Stuart Atkinson

Web site adviser: Lisa Watts
Editorial assistant: Valerie Modd

Managing designer: Ruth Russell
Managing editor: Judy Tatchell

INTERNET LINKS

If you have access to the Internet, you can visit the Web sites we have recommended in this book. On every page, you will find descriptions of what is on each Web site, and why they are worth visiting. Here are some of the things you can do on the recommended sites in this book:

- see satellite images of any part of the Earth
- explore the ocean depths in a deep-sea submarine
- take a virtual tour of the universe
- browse many galleries of actual pictures taken in space
- generate maps of the sky in an interactive Web planetarium
- find out all about volcanoes, including some on other planets
- create your own earthquakes

USBORNE QUICKLINKS

To visit the recommended sites in this book, go to the Usborne Quicklinks Web site, where you'll find links you can click on to take you straight to the sites. Just go to *www.usborne-quicklinks.com* and follow the simple instructions you find there.

Sometimes, Web addresses change or sites close down. We regularly review the sites listed in Quicklinks and update the links if necessary. We will provide suitable alternatives at *www.usborne-quicklinks.com* whenever possible. Occasionally, you may get a message saying that a site is unavailable. This may be a temporary problem, so try again later.

DOWNLOADABLE PICTURES

Pictures marked with the symbol ★ may be downloaded for your own personal use, for example, for homework or for a project, but may not be used for any commercial or profit-related purpose. To find these pictures, go to Usborne Quicklinks and follow the instructions there.

USING THE INTERNET

You can access most of the Web sites described in this book with a standard home computer and a Web browser (this is the software that enables you to access Web sites and view them on your computer).

Some Web sites need extra programs, called plug-ins, to play sounds or to show videos or animations. If you go to a site and you don't have the right plug-in, a message saying so will come up on the screen. There is usually a button you can click on to download the plug-in. Alternatively, go to Usborne Quicklinks and click on Net Help, where you will find links to plug-ins.

INTERNET SAFETY

Here are three important guidelines to follow to keep you safe while you are using the Internet:

- If a Web site asks you to register or log in, ask permission from your parent or guardian before typing in any information.
- Never give out personal information, such as your home address or phone number.
- Never arrange to meet someone that you communicated with on the Internet.

www.usborne-quicklinks.com

Go to Usborne Quicklinks for:
- direct links to all the Web sites described in this book
- free downloadable pictures, which appear throughout this book marked with a ★ symbol

SEE FOR YOURSELF

The *See for yourself* boxes in this book contain experiments, activities or observations which we have tested. Some recommended Web sites also contain experiments, but we have not tested all of these. This book will be used by readers of different ages and abilities, so it is important that you do not tackle an experiment on your own, either from the book or the Web, that involves equipment that you do not normally use, such as a kitchen knife or stove. Instead, ask an adult to help you.

CONTENTS

This huge loop of fiery gas is called a prominence. It erupts out into space from the surface of the Sun.

EARTH AND SPACE

The Earth is unique among all the known planets, because it has a breathable atmosphere and water on its surface. This allows life to exist almost everywhere, from desert sands to the deepest oceans. In this book, you can explore not only our amazing Earth, but other planets, moons and galaxies, and the vastness of space itself.

About a third of the Earth's land surface is made up of hot, dry deserts. Their beautiful landscapes are created by a mixture of wind, heat and occasional rain. Many of Earth's natural features are made in this way.

THE UNIVERSE

The **universe** or **cosmos** is the name used to describe the collection of all matter, energy and space that exists. How the universe was created is not fully understood. Most scientists believe that it began about 15,000 million years ago with an unimaginably violent explosion known as the **Big Bang**. This idea is called the **Big Bang theory**.

After the Big Bang, the fireball spread out and the universe started to expand.

SIZE AND DISTANCE

The universe is so enormous, it is impossible to imagine. Distances across it are colossal and are usually measured in **light years**. One light year is the distance light travels in one year – that is about 9.46 trillion kilometers. Light travels 300,000 kilometers in a second.

The closest star to the Earth is the Sun. It is about 93,205,679 miles away.

Sun

Earth

A ray of light takes eight minutes to travel from the Sun to the Earth.

The universe contains billions of stars gathered together in huge collections called **galaxies**. So far, astronomers have spotted galaxies that are up to 15,000 million light years away, which gives an idea of just how vast the universe must be.

This cluster of galaxies, called Abell 2218, is about 2,000 million light years away from the Earth.

THE BIG BANG THEORY

The Big Bang created a huge fireball, which cooled and formed into tiny particles. Everything in the universe is made up of these tiny particles, called **matter**.

The particles spread out and the universe began to expand. Over time, thick clouds of hydrogen and helium gases formed. These clouds then gathered together in dense clumps.

To begin with, the universe was so dense that light could not travel far within it, so it was very dark. After a few thousand years, the temperature fell to a few thousand degrees.

Very gradually, the fog cleared. This meant that light could travel further, and the universe became as transparent as it is today. The first galaxies began to form from the dense clumps of gases.

About 10,000 million years after the Big Bang, the Sun and planets of our Solar System formed near the edge of a galaxy that would later be named the Milky Way.

The modern universe contains countless millions of stars and planets, and huge clouds of dust and gas, separated by vast areas of empty space. Even today, parts of the universe are still forming.

Thick clouds of gases collected into vast clumps of dense matter.

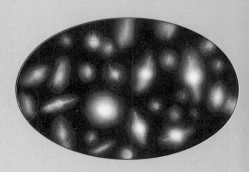

Stars and galaxies began to form. The universe became transparent as light was now able to travel through it.

Almost 10,000 million years after the Big Bang, the Solar System formed.

BIG BANG EVIDENCE

One reason why most scientists think that the Big Bang theory is correct is that a weak signal, like an echo, has been detected from space by powerful radio telescopes. It could be that this echo is from the energy in the early fireball, which spread out into space after the Big Bang.

The energy from the Big Bang explosion spread out into space.

Astronomers have calculated that if the universe contains only the matter that they know about, it would have expanded too quickly after the Big Bang for galaxies to form. This means that for the Big Bang theory to be true, the universe must contain a lot more matter than we currently know about.

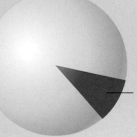

Scientists think that they only know about 10% of the universe. The rest is still to be found.

THE FUTURE

At the moment there are three main theories about the future of the universe.

The **Slowing Down theory** states that the universe could go on expanding continuously, and everything would gradually fade away. Eventually the whole universe would become just a mist of cold particles.

The universe could slow down and then simply fade away.

If more matter exists than is known about, a pulling force, called **gravity**, may eventually slow down the expansion of the universe. It will pull everything back until the galaxies crash. There could then be a Big Crunch, like the Big Bang in reverse. This idea is known as the **Big Crunch theory**.

The galaxies could collide in a Big Crunch.

When you look at the night sky, you are looking out upon millions and millions of stars.

Some scientists think that the universe works like a heart, beating in rhythm. They believe that it expands, then shrinks, then expands again, and so on. So a Big Bang is followed by a Big Crunch, in a repeating cycle. This idea is called the **Oscillating Universe theory**.

Big Bang   Big Crunch   Big Bang

Internet links

• Go to www.usborne-quicklinks.com for a link to the **Virtual Journey into the Universe Web site**, to take a superb interactive virtual tour of the Solar System.

• Go to www.usborne-quicklinks.com for a link to the **BrainPop Web site**, and watch a movie about the Big Bang theory.

• Go to www.usborne-quicklinks.com for a link to **NASA's Origins Web site**, where you can discover the mysteries of the universe and life beyond Earth.

• Go to www.usborne-quicklinks.com for a link to the **SEDS Web site**, where you can see images of objects in deep space.

• Go to www.usborne-quicklinks.com for a link to the **StarChild Web site**, a good place to learn about the universe.

GALAXIES

Stars are grouped together in vast collections called **galaxies**. Each galaxy contains billions of stars. Galaxies are themselves generally grouped together. Our Solar System forms a tiny part of a galaxy called the **Milky Way** in a group called the **Local Group**. This contains about 30 galaxies and stretches across five million light years*.

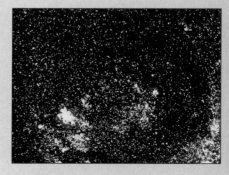

The Cartwheel galaxy is 500 million light years away.

STAR CLUSTERS

Inside galaxies, stars often group together in clusters. Stars within a cluster move at the same speed and in the same direction. There are two types of star clusters.

Open clusters are found in areas of space that are rich in gas and dust. They contain from a few dozen to a thousand bright young stars which are scattered loosely in the cluster.

This is an open cluster of stars called the Pleiades. *

Globular clusters are much larger than open clusters. They contain up to a million stars, densely packed together in sphere-shaped clumps.

Globular clusters like this one appear like very faint stars to the naked eye. *

TYPES OF GALAXIES

Galaxies form in different shapes. The four most common shapes are spiral, barred spiral, elliptical and irregular.

A **spiral galaxy** has a bright middle and two or more curved arms of stars.

A **barred spiral galaxy** has a central bar of stars with an arm at each end.

Elliptical galaxies vary in shape from round to oval. They contain many old, red stars.

An **irregular galaxy** is a cloud of stars with no definite shape. *

One third of all known galaxies are spiral shaped. Using sophisticated telescopes, astronomers have recently found new galaxies which are bigger and less tightly packed with stars than any they have seen before. These galaxies do not give off much light, so they are known as **low surface brightness galaxies**.

CARTWHEEL GALAXY

The Cartwheel galaxy (shown above) is an enormous galaxy, 150,000 light years across. Its rare shape was formed when a smaller galaxy smashed into it.

The outer ring is an immense circle of billions of new stars. These formed from the gas and dust which expanded from the core after the collision. Its original spiral shape is now starting to re-form.

NEAREST GALAXIES

The galaxies closest to our Milky Way are the Large and Small Magellanic Clouds. These are small, irregular galaxies. The nearest large galaxy is the spiral Andromeda galaxy. It is over 2.5 million light years away, and is the most distant object that can be seen with the eye on its own.

The Large Magellanic Cloud is one of the closest galaxies to the Milky Way.

* Light years, 8.

THE MILKY WAY

Compared with other galaxies, the Milky Way is relatively large, measuring about 100,000 light years across. The Earth and the rest of our Solar System lie about 32,000 light years from the middle of the Milky Way.

Most astronomers believe that the Milky Way is a spiral galaxy, although some describe it as a barred spiral galaxy. It gets its name because in ancient times, people thought that it looked like a trail of spilled milk in the night sky.

The Earth and the Solar System are here in the Milky Way.

The Milky Way

This is one of at least 150 huge globular star clusters which hover above or below the middle of the galaxy.

Areas of glowing pink, blue and green gases are nebulae, the regions where new stars form. For more about nebulae, see page 12.

See for yourself

On a clear night you could look for the Milky Way. In the northern hemisphere, the best time to see it is between July and September, although it also looks impressive on dark midwinter nights.

In the southern hemisphere, the Milky Way is at its most spectacular between October and December. It looks like a band of glowing light.

Like all spiral galaxies, the Milky Way rotates slowly. Closer to the middle it spins faster than at its edges. Our Solar System is thought to revolve around the middle of the galaxy about once every 225 million years. According to this theory, the Milky Way has rotated only once since the dinosaurs were living on the Earth.

This side view of the Milky Way shows that it has a bulge in the middle, like two fried eggs placed back to back.

Internet links

• Go to **www.usborne-quicklinks.com** for a link to the **Discovery Web site**, to travel at the speed of light, tour the Milky Way, and look back in time.

• Go to **www.usborne-quicklinks.com** for a link to the **Kapili Web site**, for a simple introduction to galaxies.

• Go to **www.usborne-quicklinks.com** for a link to the **The Online Planetarium Show Web site**, to find out about Edwin Hubble, his work and his famous telescope.

• Go to **www.usborne-quicklinks.com** for a link to the **Galaxies Web site**, to find lots of galaxy nformation and images.

• Go to **www.usborne-quicklinks.com** for a link to the **Cosmic Quest Web site**, where you can design a space station and meet famous astronomers.

STARS

Every galaxy in the universe contains millions and millions of stars. A **star** is a ball of tremendously hot gas, which produces heat and light from nuclear reactions within its core. The closest star to the Earth is the Sun, which is 93 million miles away. The second closest star is Proxima Centauri, 4.5 light years* away.

NEBULAE

Stars are formed in huge clouds of dust and gas called **nebulae**. Some nebulae are bright and some are dark. **Dark nebulae** look like dark patches in the sky. They are made mostly of dust, which blots out the light of stars behind them. The gases in **bright nebulae** are so hot that they glow in beautiful colors.

The Horse's Head Nebula is a dark nebula. It is silhouetted against a bright nebula.

The colors in a bright nebula depend on the types of gases it contains. For example, hydrogen glows pink, while oxygen glows green-blue.

The Trifid Nebula is a bright nebula. Its colors are caused by hot, glowing gases.

These columns of gas and dust, known as the Pillars of Creation, are part of the Eagle Nebula. The taller column measures about a light year from base to tip.

THE BIRTH OF A STAR

The clouds of gases and dust in some nebulae swirl around and form into clumps which grow larger and larger. Eventually, something causes these new clouds to collapse. Astronomers think this might happen when they pass through the arms of a spiral galaxy, or that the collapse is caused by a shock wave from an exploding star.

As each cloud collapses, the temperature inside it rises. After tens of thousands of years of collapse, a hot core forms. The core gets hotter and hotter until nuclear reactions begin inside, making the cloud of gases, now a star, start to shine.

Gases and dust in the nebula swirl around.

The clouds collapse.

A hot core forms.

A new star is born.

* Light years, 8.

VARIABLE STARS

Some stars appear to change occasionally in brilliance. These are called **variable stars** and they fall into three main types – pulsating, eclipsing and cataclysmic variables.

Pulsating variables are usually larger than the Sun. They change in size and temperature, giving off more light when large and less light when small. Some variable stars shrink and grow in a regular cycle, but others are more erratic. The series of pictures below shows Mira, a pulsating variable star with a regular cycle.

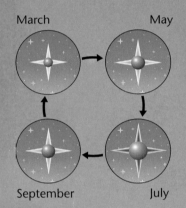

March   May

September   July

An **eclipsing variable (EcV)** is a type of **binary star**. A binary is actually two stars which orbit around each other, held in place by gravity. In an EcV, one star passes behind the other, as seen from Earth, so the brightness changes. The diagram below shows an EcV with a small, bright star and a larger, dimmer one.

An eclipsing variable

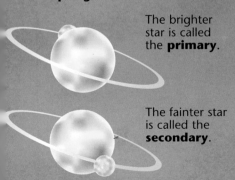

The brighter star is called the **primary**.

The fainter star is called the **secondary**.

Cataclysmic variables are binary stars that are very close together. When the gravity of one of them (usually a white dwarf*) pulls material away from the other (usually a red giant*), a huge and sudden increase in brightness occurs between and around them. This is caused by violent nuclear reactions.

One type of cataclysmic variable, called a **nova**, flares suddenly, then fades back to its original brightness. It does this over several months or even years.

THE LIFE OF A STAR

At first, most new stars burn very brightly, appearing either blue or white. They exist in this state for millions of years. As a star gets older, it shines less brightly but more steadily.

The lifespan of a star varies. Stars such as our Sun have a lifespan of about 10,000 million years. Stars smaller than the Sun, called **dwarf stars**, live longer. Stars that are larger than our Sun are **giant stars**. The biggest stars of all are **supergiant stars**. They have short lives of only a few million years.

Four bright stars

Here is a comparison of the sizes and colors of some stars. You can find out more about star colors over the page.

Arcturus is an orange giant star.

Rigel is a blue supergiant star.

See for yourself

If you look up at the sky on a clear night, you will notice that some stars seem to twinkle.

This happens because starlight passing through the Earth's atmosphere is bent and broken up. The angle at which it bends depends on the temperature of the air. The light passes through both warm and cold air, so the starlight shines at you from different directions at once, making it appear to flicker.

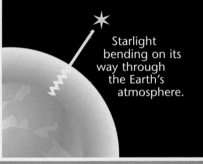

Starlight bending on its way through the Earth's atmosphere.

Barnard's Star is a red dwarf star, cooler than our Sun.

The Sun is a yellow star.

Internet links

• Go to **www.usborne-quicklinks.com** for a link to **NASA's Observatorium Web site**, to find out what stars are made of, what makes them shine, how long they live and why they are important to us.

• Go to **www.usborne-quicklinks.com** for a link to **National Geographic's Star Web site** for facts, images and a star chart.

• Go to **www.usborne-quicklinks.com** for a link to the **CurrentSky Web site**, an online newsletter for sky watchers.

• Go to **www.usborne-quicklinks.com** for a link to the **Fourmilab Web site**, where you can see sky maps and use a virtual telescope.

• Go to **www.usborne-quicklinks.com** for a link to the **SEDS Web site** and take a virtual trip around some amazing nebulae.

Red giant, White dwarf, 15.

DESCRIBING STARS

Stars burn with different amounts of brightness. Star brightness is measured on a scale called **magnitude**. The actual brilliance of a star in space is its **absolute magnitude**. A star's brightness seen from the Earth is its **apparent magnitude**. The brightest stars are classed as 0 or even minus magnitude.

Magnitude scale

-1 0 1 2 3 4 5 6 7 8 9

Brightest stars   Dimmest stars

Stars are classified by their color. The youngest, hottest stars are usually blue or white, and the coldest, oldest ones are red. A class of stars is called a **spectral type**. The main spectral types are shown in the chart below.

SPECTRAL TYPE	COLOR	EXAMPLES	TEMPERATURE

O — Blue — Zeta Orionis — 35,000°C / 62,032°F

B — Bluish-white — Spica Achernar — 21,000°C

A — White — Altair Sirius — 10,000°C / 18,032°F

F — Yellowish-white — Canopus Procyon — 7,500°C / 13,532°F

G — Yellow — Sun Capella — 6,000°C / 10,832°F

K — Orange — Aldebaran Pollux — 4,700°C / 8,492°F

M — Red — Arcturus Antares — 3,300°C / 5,972°F

CONSTELLATIONS

Since earliest times, people have noticed patterns of bright stars in the sky. These patterns are called **constellations**. There are 88 constellations visible from the Earth. Many of them are named after characters or objects taken from ancient Greek myths.

Within constellations, there are smaller patterns called **asterisms**. The Plough, or Big Dipper, is a famous asterism. It is part of the constellation Ursa Major.

The constellation of Ursa Major, or the Great Bear. Here, the imaginary shape of a bear is drawn around it.

The seven stars of the tail and hips make the asterism called the Big Dipper.

The constellations are made up of the most prominent stars in the sky. From the Earth, the stars in a constellation may look quite close to one another. In reality, they are extremely far apart. The stars in the constellation Orion, for example, vary between less than 500 light years* and over 2,000 light years away. Viewed from the Earth, the stars look like a connected group, as they lie in the same direction.

The stars in Orion look close together and the same distance from the Earth.

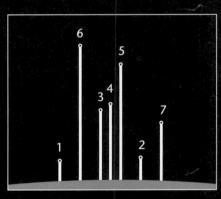

Here you can see that Orion's stars lie at very different distances from the Earth.

See for yourself

All constellations and asterisms can be seen with the naked eye, though what you can see depends on the time of year and your geographical position. Next time you are outside on a clear night, see if you can spot the Big Dipper in the northern hemisphere, or the four stars that make the Southern Cross in the southern hemisphere.

*Light years, 8.

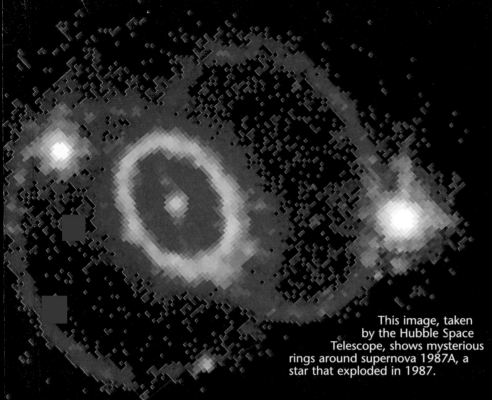

This image, taken by the Hubble Space Telescope, shows mysterious rings around supernova 1987A, a star that exploded in 1987.

BLACK HOLES

When the very biggest stars die, they form red supergiants, then explode into a supernova. However, when they collapse, they shrink so much that they virtually vanish from the universe. They may become what are called **black holes** – bottomless pits from which nothing escapes.

A black hole is so heavy and dense that its gravity sucks everything inside it, even light. This means that it cannot be seen. Anything that goes into a black hole is likely to be crushed. Some scientists think that in the middle of our galaxy lies an enormous black hole, surrounded by a mass of ancient red stars.

A ring of cool gas around a suspected black hole, as pictured by the Hubble Space Telescope*.

THE DEATH OF A STAR

Eventually a star's supply of gas runs out and it dies. As it dies, a star the size of our Sun swells up and turns red. At this stage it is called a **red giant**.

Slowly it puffs its outer layers of gas into space, leaving behind a small, most dead star called a **white dwarf**. This is about the size of a planet and is extremely dense and heavy for its size. (Imagine a golf ball that weighs as much as a truck.) The white dwarf gradually cools and fades.

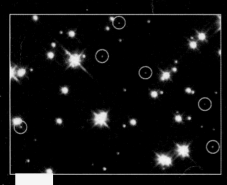

The Hubble Space Telescope* image shows six white dwarf stars (shown in circles) surrounded by yellow, Sun-like stars and cooler, red dwarf stars*.

SUPERNOVAS

Giant stars* have a really spectacular death. First they swell into vast red stars, called **red supergiants**. Then they blow up with a colossal explosion, called a **supernova**.

The supernova leaves a rapidly expanding layer of gases and dust with a small, spinning star in the middle. This is a **neutron star**. It is even denser and heavier than a white dwarf (see left). (Imagine a golf ball that weighs as much as a skyscraper.)

Some neutron stars send out beams of radiation that swing around as the star spins. These stars are called **pulsars**.

When a star dies in a huge supernova explosion, only its dense core may survive.

Pulsars are neutron stars which spin rapidly and flash like lighthouses.

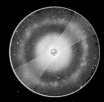

Internet links

• Go to **www.usborne-quicklinks.com** for a link to **NASA's Observatorium Web site**, to find out about the birth of stars.

• Go to **www.usborne-quicklinks.com** for a link to the **Earth and Sky Web site**, to see what's in the sky tonight.

• Go to **www.usborne-quicklinks.com** to visit the **Mystery of Space: Stars Web site**, a virtual planetarium

• Go to **www.usborne-quicklinks.com** for a link to the **Black Holes and Beyond Web site** for interesting black hole info.

• Go to **www.usborne-quicklinks.com** for a link to the **Peoria Astronomical Society Web site**. Click on the name of each constellation for a star map and description, then scroll down for images.

* Dwarf stars, Giant stars, 13; Hubble Space Telescope, 29.

THE SUN

Like all stars, the **Sun** is a massive ball of exploding gas. Although it is only a medium-sized star, life on Earth could not exist without the heat and light it provides. It also applies a huge pulling force called **gravity** to everything within 373 million miles. This is why planets, moons and other objects travel around or **orbit** the Sun.

Although the Sun is larger than everything else in the Solar System put together, it is only a medium-sized star.

INSIDE THE SUN

Within the Sun, atoms of hydrogen are continually split apart. The pieces fuse together in a different structure to make a light gas called helium. This process, called a **nuclear fusion reaction**, gives out massive amounts of energy.

Structure of the Sun

1. The Sun's **core** is 27 times wider than the Earth, and has a temperature of over 27 million degrees Fahrenheit.

2. The **radiative zone** surrounds the core. Heat produced in the core spreads through this part in waves.

3. The **convective zone** carries the Sun's energy up to the surface. The red arrows on the diagram show its churning motion.

4. The **photosphere** is the Sun's "surface". It is made of churning gases.

SURFACE OF THE SUN

Sunspots are small, dark patches on the Sun's surface which are slightly cooler than their surroundings. Clouds of glowing gas called **faculae** often surround sunspots. Huge loops of gas, called **prominences**, leap from the surface at up to 373 miles per second. Explosions called **solar flares** are even more violent and spectacular.

ECLIPSES

The Moon occasionally passes between the Earth and the Sun, blocking its light. This is called a **total solar eclipse**. The Moon can cover the Sun because although it is much smaller, it is also closer to us. If you close one eye and hold up a coin between your face and a ceiling light, you can see how this works.

During a total solar eclipse, a thin layer of gas around the Sun, called the **corona**, can be seen.

AURORAS

The Sun blows a constant stream of invisible particles out into space, in all directions. This is called the **solar wind**. When particles become trapped near the Earth's Poles, they create a dazzling light display called an **aurora**. In the north, this is called the **aurora borealis**, or **northern lights**. In the south, it is called the **aurora australis**, or **southern lights**.

See for yourself

You should never look directly at the Sun, as even glimpsing it could blind you. But there is a simple way in which you can see it indirectly.

Point a pair of binoculars at the Sun with a piece of white cardboard behind them. Move the binoculars around until a white circle appears on the cardboard, then focus them until the image is sharp. You may see dark smudges on the image. These are sunspots.

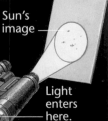

Sun's image

Keep cover on this lens.

Light enters here.

THE SOLAR SYSTEM

Together, the Sun and everything that orbits it is called the Solar System. It includes planets, moons, chunks of rock, metal and icy debris, and huge amounts of dust.

After the Sun, the most important members of the Solar System are its planets – Mercury, Venus, Earth, Mars, Jupiter, Saturn, Uranus, Neptune and Pluto. They all orbit the Sun at different distances and speeds, spinning as they do so.

A planet's **day** is the length of time it takes to make a complete 360° turn. An Earth day, for example, lasts 24 hours. A planet's **year** is the length of time it takes to orbit the Sun. The Earth's year is 365.3 days long.

Many of the planets in the Solar System have smaller companions, called **moons,** orbiting them. Moons vary greatly in size, shape and number. For instance, Earth has only one, but Saturn has at least 18. You can find out more about Earth's moon on page 21.

Earth's moon is a rocky, dusty ball.

Large lumps of rock and metal called **asteroids**, and chunks of frozen gas and dirt called **comets,** also orbit the Sun. Most asteroids are found between Mars and Jupiter, but a comet's orbit may be in any part of the Solar System. You can find out more about asteroids and comets on pages 26-27.

The Solar System

Below, you can see the nine planets in the Solar System. The distances between them are not shown to scale because they are too vast.

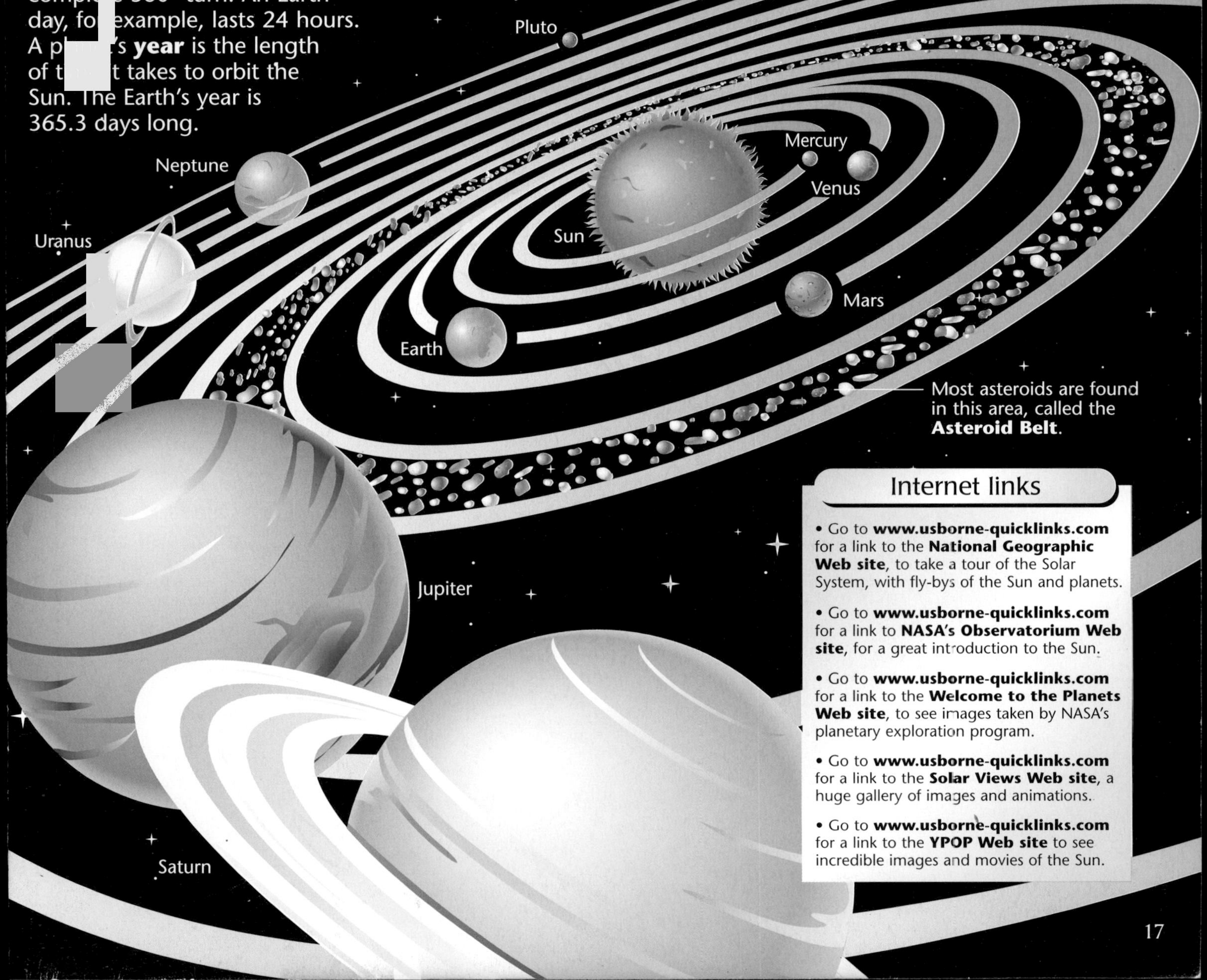

Pluto

Neptune

Uranus

Sun

Mercury

Venus

Mars

Earth

Jupiter

Saturn

Most asteroids are found in this area, called the **Asteroid Belt**.

Internet links

• Go to **www.usborne-quicklinks.com** for a link to the **National Geographic Web site**, to take a tour of the Solar System, with fly-bys of the Sun and planets.

• Go to **www.usborne-quicklinks.com** for a link to **NASA's Observatorium Web site**, for a great introduction to the Sun.

• Go to **www.usborne-quicklinks.com** for a link to the **Welcome to the Planets Web site**, to see images taken by NASA's planetary exploration program.

• Go to **www.usborne-quicklinks.com** for a link to the **Solar Views Web site**, a huge gallery of images and animations.

• Go to **www.usborne-quicklinks.com** for a link to the **YPOP Web site** to see incredible images and movies of the Sun.

THE INNER PLANETS

Mercury, Venus, Earth and Mars are known as the inner planets. This is because they are the closest planets to the Sun. Although they all have a similar small size and rocky structure, only Earth is the right distance from the Sun for life to exist on its surface. You can find out more about Earth on pages 20-21.

The diagram above shows the four inner planets and their orbits around the Sun.

MERCURY

Mercury is a very small planet, with a diameter of only 3,032 miles. It is the closest planet to the Sun, orbiting it at a distance of about 24 million miles. This closeness means that Mercury is blasted by the Sun's rays. Its daytime temperature can reach 800°F, which is over four times hotter than boiling water.

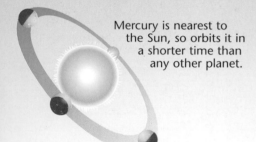

Mercury is nearest to the Sun, so orbits it in a shorter time than any other planet.

It takes Mercury 88 Earth days to orbit the Sun. As it travels, it spins slowly. In fact, each day on Mercury is equal to 58.7 Earth days. This means that there are fewer than two days in one Mercury year. So during its long night, when half of the planet faces away from the Sun, the temperature can plummet as low as -297°F.

VENUS

Venus, the second planet from the Sun, is a similar size to the Earth. It orbits the Sun at a distance of about 67 million miles. The planet's surface is mainly flat, but it has raised areas which look like Earth's continents.

Venus has an atmosphere that is mostly made up of carbon dioxide gas. It presses down on the planet's surface like a great weight. Dense clouds of sulfuric acid reflect the Sun's rays, making Venus shine like a very bright star. Any rays which are not reflected become trapped around the planet, raising its temperature to around 900°F.

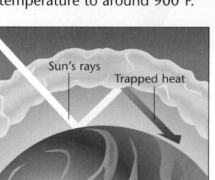

Sun's rays

Trapped heat

Venus's thick atmosphere acts like the glass in a greenhouse. Any rays that travel through it become trapped.

This computer-colored image shows dense clouds swirling around Venus.

See for yourself

You can try spotting the inner planets yourself. Mercury and Venus can sometimes be seen just before sunrise and just after sunset. After the Sun and Moon, Venus is the brightest object in the sky. It is often called the **Morning Star** or the **Evening Star**, depending on what time of day it appears. Mercury looks like a bright star close to the horizon.

CAUTION
When you are planet spotting, always make sure that the Sun has not begun to rise in the morning or has fully set in the evening. Glimpsing the Sun's rays might damage your eyes.

STUDYING VENUS

Nobody knew what the surface of Venus looked like until 1975, when two space probes named Venera were sent by the Soviet Union. Smaller probes were dropped from them. Their cameras revealed that the surface of Venus was covered with sharp rocks and looked like a gloomy, orange-brown desert.

Venus's surface has shallow craters. Objects cannot strike with enough force to make deep craters because the atmosphere slows them down.

In the late 1980s and early 1990s, an American space probe named Magellan used radar to map the planet's surface in greater detail. It was found to be covered mostly by areas of solidified lava, which had flowed out of Venus's many volcanoes.

Magellan space probe

The picture below is a computer image of Venus's surface. It was created using information collected by the Magellan probe.

MARS

Mars is the fourth planet from the Sun. It is just half the size of the Earth and orbits the Sun at a distance of about 142 million miles, taking just under 687 days to do so.

Mars is sometimes called the **Red Planet**, because of the reddish dust covering its surface.

Mars has two moons, called **Phobos** and **Deimos**, which are dark and dusty. Many scientists think that these odd-shaped moons are really asteroids that became trapped in orbit around Mars millions of years ago.

Deimos, Mars's smaller moon, is about 9 miles across at its widest.

Phobos is 17 miles across at its widest. It has a large crater named Stickney on its surface which is about 3 miles across.

STUDYING THE SURFACE

In the 1960s and 1970s, the Mariner and Viking space probes sent back detailed pictures of the surface of Mars. It was shown to be covered in reddish-orange dust, with many rocky canyons and craters. Huge dust storms, which may last for weeks, often rage across the landscape.

The most recent successful Mars missions, called Mars Pathfinder and Mars Global Surveyor, were launched in 1996. The Pathfinder mission is now over, but the Surveyor craft will continue to send information and images from Mars for a few more years.

The Pathfinder spacecraft carried this tiny vehicle named Sojourner, which roamed over the planet's surface, studying and photographing rocks.

Internet links

• Go to **www.usborne-quicklinks.com** for links to the **SEDS Web site** to learn about the inner planets and their moons.

• Go to **www.usborne-quicklinks.com** for a link to the **Windows to the Universe Web site**, where you'll find amazing information, fantastic pictures and interactive games.

• Go to **www.usborne-quicklinks.com** for a link to the **Destination Mars Web site**, where you can find an animated introduction to Martian geography, geology, weather and more.

• Go to **www.usborne-quicklinks.com** for a link to **NASA's Observatorium Web site**, to read fascinating stories about Mars and find out about missions to the planet.

THE EARTH AND MOON

The **Earth** orbits the Sun at a distance of about 93 million miles. This distance makes it just the right temperature for water to exist as a liquid, rather than just ice or vapor. The Earth also has a breathable atmosphere. All these things create the right conditions for life to exist.

The Earth as seen from space. Early astronauts described it as a beautiful blue jewel.

EARTH'S ATMOSPHERE

From space, the Earth's atmosphere looks like a very thin blue layer surrounding the planet. It is a mixture of nitrogen and oxygen, with traces of other gases. It contains more oxygen than the atmosphere of any other planet. This gas is vital to life.

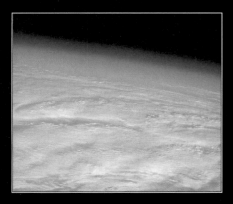

From space, the Earth's atmosphere looks like a thin haze. It appears blue because of the way sunlight is filtered through atmospheric gases.

EARTH'S SURFACE

Beneath the atmosphere is the planet's surface, called the **crust**. This is split into a number of enormous slabs called plates*, which have pushed and pulled against each other for millions of years, creating mountains, valleys and other features.

Mountain ranges like the Himalayas formed when the Earth's vast plates crushed together.

Two-thirds of the Earth's surface is covered in vast oceans of water. These are believed to be the birthplace of Earth's first life-forms, around 3,500 million years ago. Scientists study other planets and moons for signs of water or ice on their surface. This could show that they are or were once home to primitive life.

THE EARTH FROM SPACE

Today, people are learning more and more about the Earth, from information sent back by satellites and space stations. For instance, weather forecasters use data collected by satellites to predict weather patterns. They can use this information to warn people of severe weather anywhere in the world.

Information from satellites is also used to find out more about the Earth's surface. Even areas that are normally hard to see, such as the ocean floor, can now be seen in detail using sophisticated satellites.

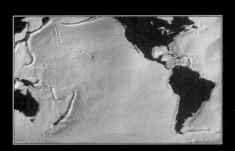

This map of the ocean floor was produced by a satellite named Seasat. The dark shapes are continents.

The Earth is the only planet in the Solar System which is definitely known to support life. This is because it is mostly covered in water, which has yet to be found on any other planet's surface.

*Plates, 35.

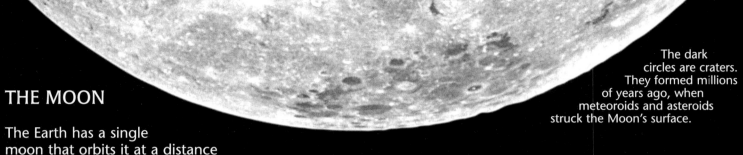

The dark circles are craters. They formed millions of years ago, when meteoroids and asteroids struck the Moon's surface.

THE MOON

The Earth has a single moon that orbits it at a distance of about 238,855 miles. Most moons are tiny compared to the objects they orbit, but our **Moon** is a quarter of the Earth's size.

The Moon is kept in orbit by the pull of the Earth's gravity.

Because of the Earth's gravity, the same side of the Moon always faces us as it orbits. The other side of the Moon, known as the **far** or **dark side**, has only been seen by space probes and astronauts.

Unlike the Earth, the Moon has no atmosphere to prevent it from becoming too hot or too cold. This means that the Sun's rays can make its temperature rise to 253°F. When the Sun is not shining on the Moon, the temperature can fall to -261°F.

See for yourself

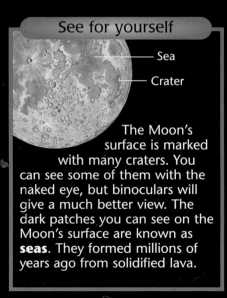

Sea

Crater

The Moon's surface is marked with many craters. You can see some of them with the naked eye, but binoculars will give a much better view. The dark patches you can see on the Moon's surface are known as **seas**. They formed millions of years ago from solidified lava.

PHASES OF THE MOON

The Moon does not make its own light, but it reflects the Sun's rays. This can make it look very bright in the night sky. Different amounts of the Moon's sunlit side can be seen as it orbits the Earth. This makes the Moon appear to change shape each night. The different shapes are called the **phases** of the Moon.

It takes 28 days for the Moon to orbit the Earth once. The diagram below shows the Moon's phases during this time.

The phases of the Moon

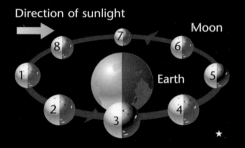

Direction of sunlight

Moon

Earth

The pictures below show what the Moon looks like from the Earth when it is in each of the numbered positions shown above.

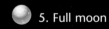 1. New moon   5. Full moon

 2. Crescent   6. Waning (becoming smaller)

 3. Half moon   7. Half moon

 4. Waxing (becoming larger)   8. Crescent

THE MOON'S FORMATION

Scientists are still not completely sure where the Moon came from. They used to think it was formed at the same time as the Earth, but studies of Moon rocks seem to show that this is not the case.

Most astronomers now think that the Moon was formed when a massive object, the size of a small planet, collided with the Earth. This threw out an enormous amount of rocky debris, which joined together in a single mass to form the Moon.

Large object ————

Earth ————

The Moon may have formed from rocky debris thrown out after a huge object smashed into the Earth.

Moon ————

Internet links

• Go to **www.usborne-quicklinks.com** for a link to the **Fourmilab Web site** to see incredible live satellite pictures of the Earth and Moon. You can zoom in on the areas you want to see more closely.

• Go to **www.usborne-quicklinks.com** for a link to the **Windows to the Universe Web site**, where you can find out all about the Earth and its atmosphere, magnetosphere, ecosystems and moon.

• Go to **www.usborne-quicklinks.com** for a link to the **Planetscapes Web site**, where you can find Earth and Moon facts, and see animations and images.

THE OUTER PLANETS

Jupiter, Saturn, Uranus, Neptune and Pluto are known as the **outer planets**. They lie in the outer regions of the Solar System. Except for tiny, rocky Pluto, all of these planets are huge balls made almost entirely of gas, so they are sometimes called the **gas giants**.

The Galileo space probe has been studying Jupiter since 1995.

JUPITER

Jupiter is the largest planet in the Solar System, measuring 88,846 miles at its equator. It takes about 11.9 Earth years to orbit the Sun once. Despite its distance from the Sun, Jupiter is not a frozen planet. Pressurized hydrogen at its heart breaks down to create huge amounts of heat.

Several space probes have been sent to Jupiter. In 1979 the Voyager probes discovered that Jupiter has faint rings, which cannot be seen from the Earth.

In 1995, the Galileo space probe took a new series of photos, and also sent a mini-probe down into Jupiter's atmosphere. It discovered that Jupiter's winds blew harder than any on Earth, and gathered more information on the planet's rings and moons.

JUPITER'S MOONS

So far, astronomers have discovered 17 moons in orbit around Jupiter. The four largest are called the **Galilean Moons**, after the Italian scientist Galileo, who discovered them in 1610. Jupiter's other moons are much smaller. Some may be just asteroids, captured by the planet's gravity.

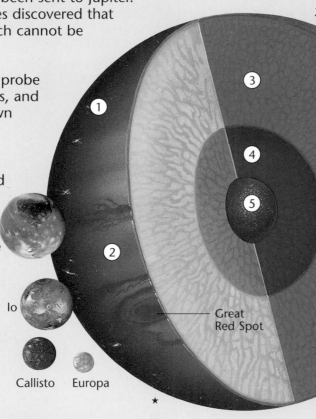

Ganymede

Io

Callisto   Europa

Great Red Spot

The Galilean Moons (not shown to scale above)

Ganymede is the largest moon in the Solar System. It is even bigger than the planet Mercury.

Io is covered with volcanoes that pour sulfur onto its surface.

Callisto is a ball of dusty ice. Its surface is scarred with hundreds of craters.

Europa may have a deep ocean beneath its fractured, icy crust. Some scientists believe that this ocean may contain simple life.

Structure of Jupiter

Scientists base this idea of Jupiter's structure on information from space probes.

1. The atmosphere's top layer is broken into vast clouds by high winds. Violent storms rage around the planet.

2. The dark bands are gaps in the clouds. Deeper, hotter layers of the planet's churning atmosphere can be seen beneath.

3. This layer is 10,563 miles thick. It is made of hydrogen gas which is so compressed that it acts like a liquid.

4. This layer is also made of hydrogen, but it is so compressed that it behaves like a solid.

5. The core, which is slightly larger than the Earth, is thought to be solid and rocky.

See for yourself

After the Sun, Moon and Venus, Jupiter is the brightest object in the sky. With the naked eye it looks like a very bright star. If you have a telescope, you may be able to see its tinted cloud bands and the **Great Red Spot**, a vast storm which rages through the planet's atmosphere.

SATURN

Saturn is the second largest planet in the Solar System. It measures about 74,898 miles around its equator – nine times wider than the Earth. Saturn orbits the Sun once every 29.5 Earth years, at a distance of about 888 million miles.

The planet is made up mostly of hydrogen and helium, which are very light gases. This makes Saturn very light compared to the other planets. Astronomers believe that Saturn may be similar to Jupiter on the inside, because it also generates its own fierce heat.

Saturn's rings are made of dust and rocks.

SATURN'S RINGS

Saturn is often called the **Ringed Planet**, because it is surrounded by rings of dust and rocks. These were identified in the seventeenth century by Galileo. Space probes such as Pioneer 11 (in 1979) and the Voyagers have since sent lots of information about the rings. Scientists now know that there are other planets with rings.

Saturn's rings are just under one mile thick and are made up of dust, rocks and icy boulders. The rings that can be seen from the Earth are actually made up of thousands of smaller **ringlets**. The outer ring particles are kept in place by the gravity of two small moons, known as the **Shepherd Moons**.

SATURN'S MOONS

Saturn has 18 moons, some of which are shown on the right. Scientists think that Saturn's and Jupiter's moons are among the places in the Solar System where evidence of simple life is most likely to be found.

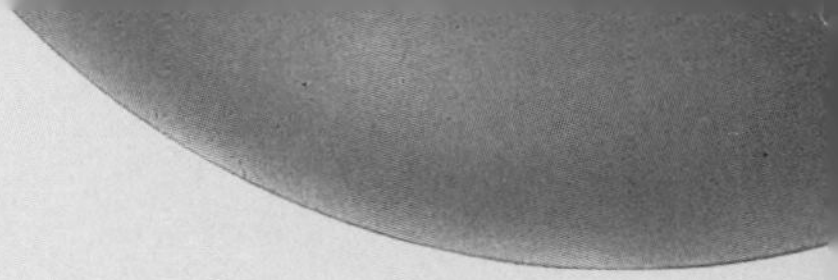

Saturn is the second largest planet in the Solar System. It is about nine times the size of the Earth.

Saturn's biggest moon, **Titan**, is surrounded by dense orange clouds.

Mimas is about 247 miles wide and heavily cratered. The impact that created its largest crater almost destroyed it completely.

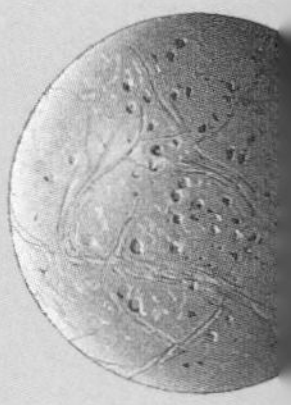

Enceladus is slightly larger than Mimas and is much smoother. Most of its craters are covered by ice.

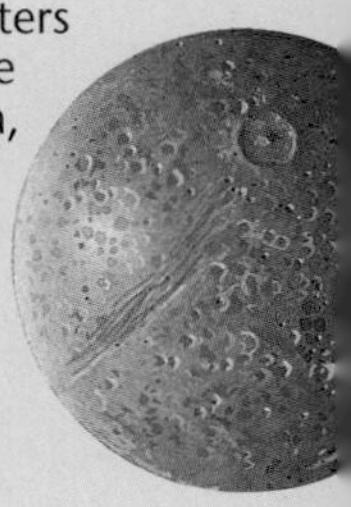

Tethys has huge craters and long valleys. The longest valley, Ithaca, is 1,243 miles. The largest crater, Odysseus, is 249 miles wide.

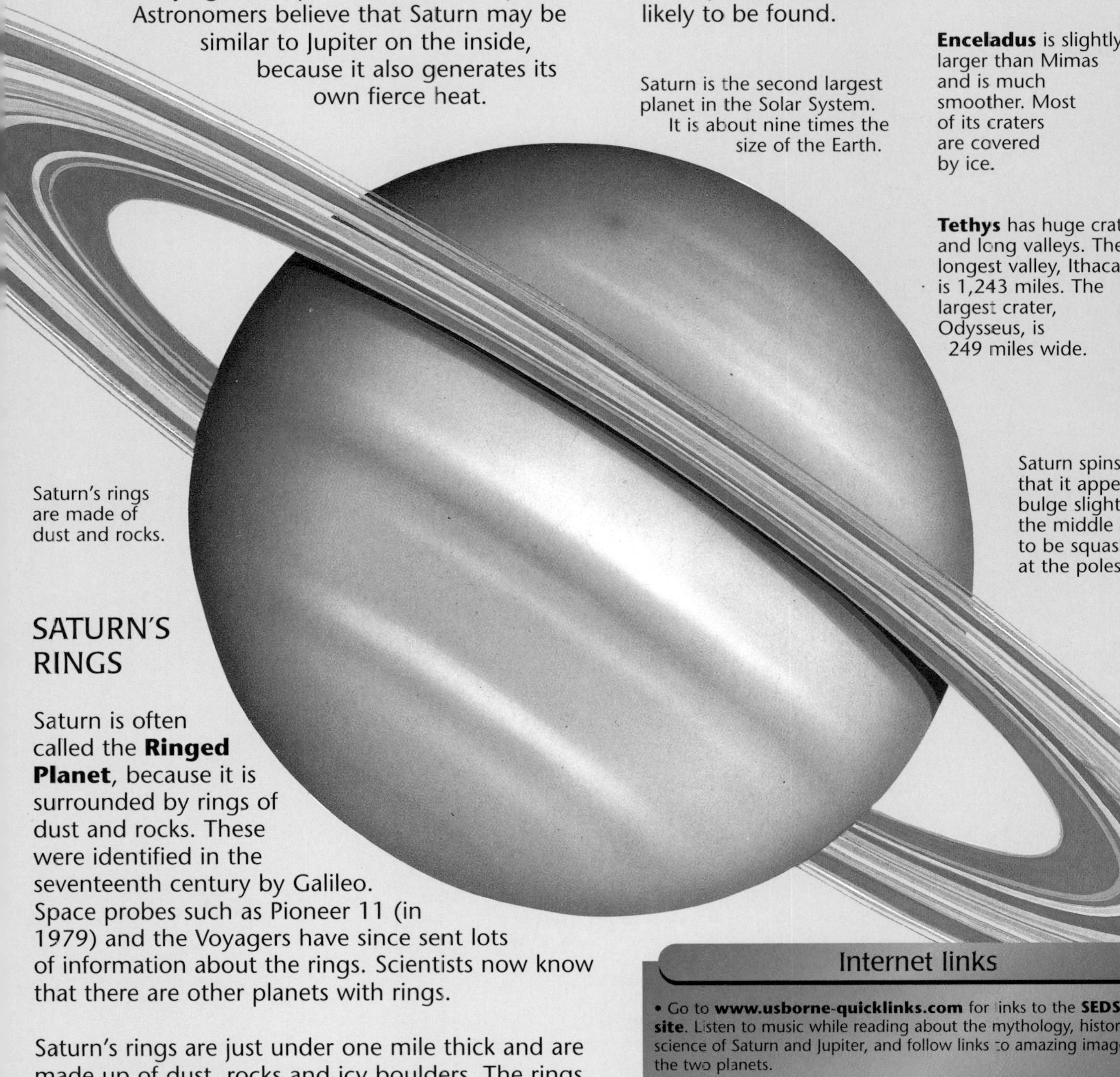

Saturn spins so fast that it appears to bulge slightly in the middle and to be squashed at the poles.

Internet links

• Go to **www.usborne-quicklinks.com** for links to the **SEDS Web site**. Listen to music while reading about the mythology, history and science of Saturn and Jupiter, and follow links to amazing images of the two planets.

• Go to **www.usborne-quicklinks.com** for links to the **Welcome to the Planets Web site**, where you can find vital statistics, essential information and incredible images of Saturn and Jupiter. You can also learn about features on their surfaces, as well as their various moons.

URANUS

Uranus was discovered by British astronomer William Herschel in 1781. It takes just over 84 Earth years to orbit the Sun, at a distance of around 1,783 million miles. It travels slowly, moving at about 4.3 miles per second. By comparison, the Earth moves at nearly 18.6 miles per second.

Most planets spin around like tops, but Uranus rolls around the Sun on its side, like a barrel. It may have been tipped onto its side millions of years ago by a collision with a planet-sized comet. Uranus spins quickly, making one turn in 17.9 hours.

Like Saturn, Uranus has a system of rings, which were discovered in 1977. In 1986, the Voyager 2 space probe photographed and measured them. The rings were found to be made up mostly of dark dust.

MOONS OF URANUS

For many years, Uranus was thought to have 15 moons. Astronomers have now officially identified at least 21, and there may be more awaiting discovery.

The five largest moons are shown below. **Ariel** and **Umbriel** are both dark and cratered, while **Titania** has deep, long valleys. **Oberon** is heavily cratered, but little else is known about it. **Miranda** is a small ball of ice, about 293 miles across. It is thought that it may once have been broken apart by a comet.

Ariel

Umbriel

Titania

Oberon

 Miranda

This picture of Uranus and its rings was created using information taken with the HST's* Near Infrared Camera. The red patches are high clouds.

A photo of Neptune, taken by the Voyager 2 space probe in 1989.

NEPTUNE

Neptune was first discovered by astronomers John Couch Adams and Urbain Jean LeVerrier. It is slightly smaller than Uranus, and spins once every 19.2 hours. Neptune is about 2,799 million miles from the Sun. It takes about 165 Earth years to complete a single orbit.

You cannot see Neptune with the naked eye, and even through a telescope it only looks like a small, bluish circle.

NEPTUNE'S ATMOSPHERE

Methane gas in the atmosphere gives Neptune its blue appearance. Neptune's atmosphere also contains ammonia and helium. Beneath its dense blanket of gases, the planet is thought to have an outer layer of liquid hydrogen.

Voyager 2 observed long, wispy clouds swirling around Neptune, blown by winds of up to 1,243 miles per hour. It also saw dark spots. The largest, named the **Great Dark Spot**, was a vast storm the size of the Earth.

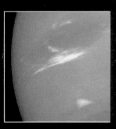

Neptune's Great Dark Spot. Voyager 2 scientists named the little cloud below it the Scooter, because it raced around the planet every 16 hours.

* HST (Hubble Space Telescope), 29.

PLUTO

Pluto is the Solar System's smallest planet, measuring just 1,420 miles across. It was first discovered in 1930 by American astronomer Clyde Tombaugh. Pluto has an oval orbit, so its distance from the Sun varies a great deal. Most of the time Pluto is the furthest planet in the Solar System. At its closest, it is about 2,749 million miles from the Sun. At its furthest, it is about 4,582 million miles away. It takes 248 years to orbit the Sun once.

Although Pluto is currently classified as a planet, some astronomers believe it may not be one. Its small size and odd orbit suggest it could actually be a huge asteroid.

Pluto has a single moon, called **Charon**, which was discovered in 1978. Charon is nearly half Pluto's size, making it unusually large for a moon. For this reason, some astronomers think that Pluto and Charon are in fact a pair of planets.

Pluto's orbit is tilted at an angle compared with the other planets. It cuts across Neptune's orbit.

NEPTUNE'S MOONS

Neptune has eight moons. The largest of them are **Triton** and **Nereid**. Triton is bigger than the planet Pluto. Most moons orbit their planet in the same direction as the planet spins. Triton, however, travels in the opposite direction, as shown in the diagram below.

Neptune spins counterclockwise.

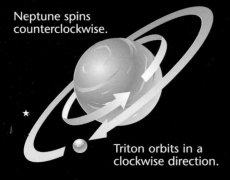

Triton orbits in a clockwise direction.

Most of Triton's surface is bright and smooth. It has some dark streaks over it and pink ice around its south pole. Triton has a thin atmosphere of nitrogen and methane.

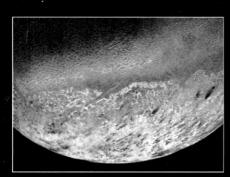

This photograph of Triton shows the polar cap. Its pink tinge may be due to the evaporation of frozen nitrogen gas.

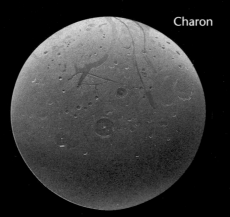

Charon

Pluto and its moon Charon are very close to each other. They are only about 12,427 miles apart.

Pluto

STUDYING PLUTO

Pluto is very hard to see, because it is so far away. Even powerful telescopes on Earth show Pluto as just a tiny circle with no surface markings. But images from the Hubble Space Telescope* suggest that it may be an icy, rocky ball like Neptune's moon, Triton, with an atmosphere of frozen methane and nitrogen.

Astronomers are keen to send a probe to Pluto, because it is the only planet yet to be explored and photographed in detail. This is a difficult task, though, as a probe would take about 12 years to get there. It is also thought that the planet's atmosphere freezes solid and falls to the surface as it moves away from the Sun. The probe would have to reach Pluto before this happened, or surface features might be hidden from view.

Internet links

• Go to **www.usborne-quicklinks.com** for links to the **SEDS Web site**. Listen to music while reading about the mythology and science of Neptune, Uranus and Pluto, and how these planets were discovered. Follow the links to see amazing images of the three planets.

• Go to **www.usborne-quicklinks.com** for a link to the **Windows to the Universe Web site**. There, you will find lots of illustrated details about Neptune, Uranus, Pluto and their moons, including discoveries made by the Voyager space missions to Neptune and Uranus.

• Go to **www.usborne-quicklinks.com** for links to the **Views of the Solar System Web site**, a useful source of information about Neptune, Uranus, Pluto and their moons.

* Hubble Space Telescope (HST), NASA (National Aeronautics Space Administration), 29.

SPACE DEBRIS

As well as many planets and moons, the Solar System also contains millions of smaller objects, called asteroids, comets and meteoroids. They are believed to be pieces of debris left over from the birth of the universe.

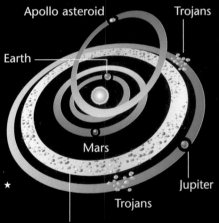

Hale-Bopp, the clearest comet to be seen for 100 years, came into view between 1995 and 1997.

ASTEROIDS

Asteroids are large pieces of rock, or rock and metal. The first was spotted in 1801, by an Italian astronomer named Piazzi. He found an object in space which he believed was a tiny planet. Piazzi named his discovery **Ceres**.

Soon, other astronomers noticed similar objects, which they called asteroids. This means "like stars". Most orbit the Sun between Mars and Jupiter, in an area called the **Asteroid Belt**.

The first close-up pictures of an asteroid were taken in 1991, by the space probe Galileo. It photographed the asteroid **Gaspra**. The images showed Gaspra to be about 12 miles across with an irregular shape. Its surface is grooved and pitted with craters.

Gaspra is one of the largest asteroids in the Asteroid Belt. It is dark reddish-brown, with patches of gray and blue.

NUMBERS AND TYPES

Several hundred thousand asteroids have already been discovered and many more are discovered every year. Most asteroids fall into one of three main groups, depending on what they are made of. These groups are carbonaceous (like Ceres), silicaceous (like Gaspra) and metallic.

Carbonaceous (or **C-type**) asteroids are the most common. They are stony and darker than coal.

Silicaceous (or **S-type**) asteroids are bright and shiny. They contain metal.

Metallic (or **M-type**) asteroids may be the exposed, metal cores of originally much larger objects.

Asteroids are often scarred with craters, made by smaller pieces of space debris colliding with them.

TROJANS AND APOLLOS

There are several other groups of asteroids besides the ones in the main Asteroid Belt. For instance, Jupiter holds clusters of asteroids in its gravity. These asteroids are called the **Trojans**. Some orbit in front of Jupiter, and others orbit behind it.

Apollo asteroid   Trojans

Earth

Mars

★   Jupiter

Trojans

Asteroid Belt

Other asteroids, known as the **Apollo asteroids**, sometimes cross the Earth's path. Their usual orbit, however, is further away from the Sun.

Although they are shown close together here, the distances between these asteroids are so huge that spacecraft can pass through without hitting any of them.

NEAR ENCOUNTER

Asteroids which closely approach the Earth are called **near-Earth asteroids**. The **NEAR** project, which stands for **Near Earth Asteroid Rendezvous**, was created to study one of these asteroids, called **Eros**. The NEAR spacecraft was launched in February 1996, and reached Eros in February 2000, to complete a one-year orbit.

Before it landed on Eros' rocky surface, NEAR took thousands of pictures of the asteroid's craters and features. Thanks to this successful mission, astronomers now know much more about the structure of near-Earth asteroids.

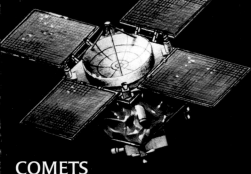

The NEAR spacecraft. Pictures from it have revealed lots of new information about near-Earth asteroids.

COMETS

Comets are balls of dirty ice. They travel around the Sun in huge, oval orbits. This means that they spend most of their time far away from the Sun. Some comets have such wide orbits that they may travel far above or below the Solar System for thousands of years. The diagram on the right shows some comets' orbits.

A COMET'S TAIL

The central, solid part of a comet is called the **nucleus**. This is made up of frozen gases, ice, grit and rock. When a comet is near to the Sun, its nucleus becomes warmer. As the comet begins to melt, a tail is formed. Some comets have more than one tail.

How a comet tail forms

This is a comet flying through space, far from the Sun. At this stage it has no tail.

As the comet approaches the Sun, it melts. Gas and dust stream out into space, forming a cloud called a **coma**.

A constant stream of particles from the Sun, called the **solar wind**, blows the coma out behind. This creates the comet's tail.

★

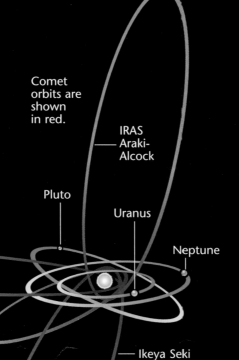

Comet orbits are shown in red.

IRAS
Araki-
Alcock

Pluto

Uranus

Neptune

Kohoutek

Halley

Ikeya Seki

METEOROIDS

Meteoroids are very small pieces of space debris. They may be grains of dust from comets, chunks of rock, or even bits of shattered asteroids.

Occasionally, the Earth crosses the path of these meteoroids. As they plummet through the atmosphere, they burn up in a streak of light. At this stage, they are called **meteors**, or **shooting stars**. Meteoroids that travel all the way through the atmosphere and land on the Earth are called **meteorites**.

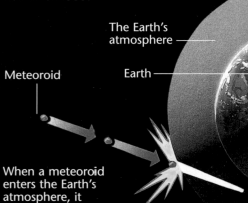

The Earth's atmosphere

Meteoroid

Earth

When a meteoroid enters the Earth's atmosphere, it becomes a meteor.

See for yourself

A **meteor shower** is a short but spectacular display of meteors caused by the Earth crossing a comet's path. Astronomy magazines and the Internet can tell you the best dates to look for showers in your hemisphere.

Internet links

• Go to **www.usborne-quicklinks.com** for a link to the **Comet's Tale Web site**, to play an interactive game, watch a slide show and read about comet origins.

• Go to **www.usborne-quicklinks.com** for a link to the **SEDS Web site** and find out more about asteroids and meteors.

• Go to **www.usborne-quicklinks.com** for a link to the **NEAR mission Web site**, for the latest NEAR information.

• Go to **www.usborne-quicklinks.com** for a link to the **Comet Hale-Bopp Web site**, for more on this famous comet.

SPACE EXPLORATION

Studying space in detail only became possible after the invention of the telescope in the seventeenth century. Since then, astronomers have used many more sophisticated devices to look further and further into space. In the twentieth century, scientists discovered how to send man-made satellites, and then people, into space to study it in even greater detail.

The first true astronomical telescope was built by Galileo in 1610. It could magnify up to nine times, but his later ones could magnify up to 30 times.

OPTICAL TELESCOPES

Optical telescopes create images using light. Some optical telescopes, called **refractors**, collect light through lenses. **Reflectors** use mirrors to collect light and reflect it back to the observer. Astronomers use vast reflector telescopes, housed in buildings called **observatories**, to look far into space.

The Keck observatories in Hawaii house the world's most powerful optical telescopes. Like many observatories, they are built on mountaintops, which are above most of the haze and pollution in the atmosphere.

This reflector telescope, Keck 1, is over 33ft wide. Its mirror is made up of 36 segments which act like a single, giant mirror.

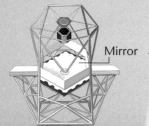
Mirror

RADIO TELESCOPES

Radio telescopes have very large dishes with moveable antennas, that collect the faint signals given out by objects in space. They allow astronomers to detect things that are too dark or too far away to see, even through the most powerful optical telescope.

The largest radio telescope is the Arecibo dish in Puerto Rico. Its 1,000ft wide dish is built into a natural valley. It is sensitive enough to detect faint signals from galaxies in distant areas of the universe. These signals are 100 million years old when they reach the Earth.

A radio telescope. It can be steered to face a particular target in space.

SPACE TELESCOPES

Telescopes that are placed out in space can see much further than telescopes on Earth, because the planet's atmosphere does not block their view. The largest telescope to have been placed in space so far is the Hubble Space Telescope (HST), an optical telescope launched by NASA (the National Aeronautics Space Administration) in 1990.

The HST's main mirror measures 8ft across.

When the HST was launched, astronomers hoped it would provide the answers to many questions about the nature and size of the universe. After its main mirror was repaired in 1993, it sent back some of the most astonishing pictures of the universe ever seen.

Galaxy M100 is tens of millions of light years away. This image was taken by the HST after its mirror was repaired.

SATELLITES

There are many man-made devices orbiting the Earth. These are known as **satellites** – the same word that is used for any object, such as a moon, which orbits a planet or star. Some man-made satellites gather and transmit information about space directly to scientists on Earth. Others pick up radio, TV or telephone signals, and send them back down to other places on Earth.

The first man-made object ever to go into space was a satellite named Sputnik 1, which was launched in 1957 by the Soviet Union. It could not take pictures or record information, but it proved that man-made structures could be launched successfully into space.

In 1989, the satellite Hipparcos was launched by the European Space Agency. For three and a half years, it mapped the night sky in the greatest detail ever. Results were published in 1997 and this new information has since allowed astronomers to calculate, with greater accuracy than ever before, how far away thousands of stars and other objects are.

This satellite orbits at the same speed as the Earth spins. This is known as a **geostationary** orbit.

This is one of NASA's Tracking and Data Relay Satellites (TDRS). They communicate with spacecraft orbiting close to the Earth.

See for yourself

If you would like to look at the stars and planets yourself, you will need a map of the night sky. Star maps in astronomy books will help you to identify the constellations, but the sky looks different from the Northern and Southern hemispheres, so you need the right map for your part of the world. If you want to spot planets, charts in the monthly astronomy magazines show which planets can be seen at a particular time.

Internet links

- Go to **www.usborne-quicklinks.com** for a link to the **Arecibo Observatory Web site** to find out more about the world's largest single-dish radio telescope.

- Go to **www.usborne-quicklinks.com** for a link to the **Keck Observatory Web site** to study its amazing telescopes.

- Go to **www.usborne-quicklinks.com** for a link to the **Space Telescope Science Institute Web site** to read the amazing story of the Hubble Telescope.

- Go to **www.usborne-quicklinks.com** for a link to the **Sea and Sky Web site**, an amateur astronomy information source.

- Go to **www.usborne-quicklinks.com** for a link to **the Tech Web site** to learn about satellites or even build one.

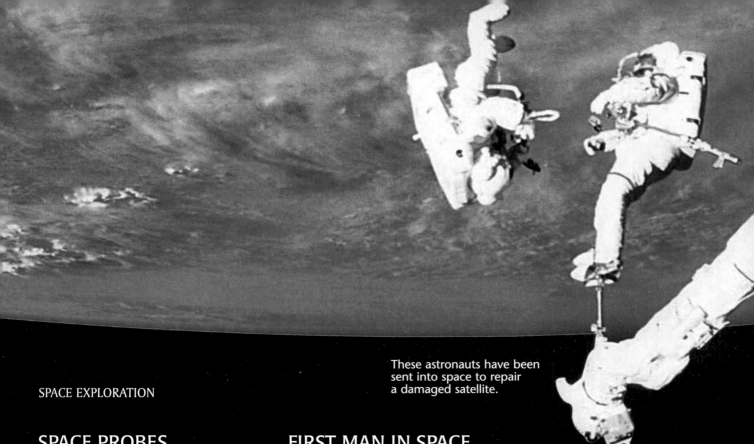

The most recent manned Moon mission was Apollo 17, in 1972.

These astronauts have been sent into space to repair a damaged satellite.

SPACE PROBES

Since the 1960s, unmanned spacecraft called **space probes** have been sent to explore the Solar System. Many carry cameras, which take detailed photographs of distant planets. They beam the pictures back to Earth, where they are studied by astronomers.

One such project was NASA's Galileo mission to Jupiter, launched in 1989. Galileo also carried a smaller probe, which split from its mother ship to study the planet's atmosphere. Recently, the Mars Pathfinder probe landed on Mars and sent a small remote-controlled vehicle to explore the surface.

So far, Pioneer 10 (which studied Jupiter and Saturn) and Pioneer 11 (which studied Saturn) have journeyed further than any other probes. After completing their missions, they drifted out of our Solar System, and are no longer active.

FIRST MAN IN SPACE

For many years, space travel was thought to be too dangerous for humans. But advances in technology throughout the 1950s led to Russian astronaut Yuri Gagarin becoming the first man in space, in 1961. His flight lasted for one and a half hours.

MEN ON THE MOON

In 1959, a Soviet space probe, Luna 9, was the first man-made object to land on the Moon. Ten years later, American astronauts Neil Armstrong and Edwin "Buzz" Aldrin traveled to the Moon in the Apollo 11 spacecraft and became the first people to walk on its surface.

During the 1960s and 1970s there were six Moon landings. Each crew collected information and rock samples. Scientists are still studying these rocks in order to understand more about how the Moon formed and evolved billions of years ago. This may also offer clues about the Earth's formation.

This is the Space Shuttle's Remote Manipulator System, a moveable "arm" which can retrieve objects and bring them into the Shuttle.

The most recent manned Moon mission was Apollo 17, in 1972.

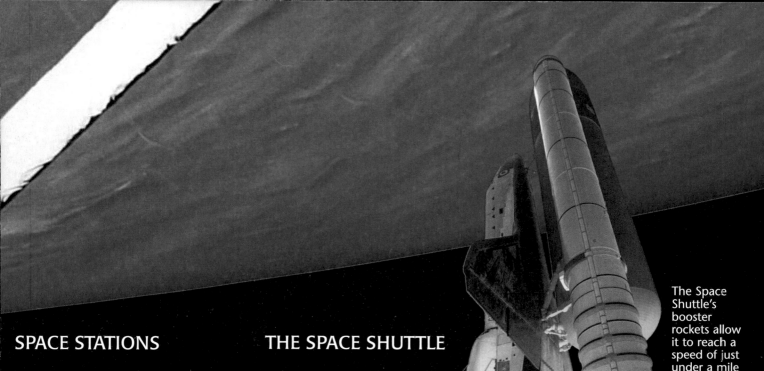

The Space Shuttle's booster rockets allow it to reach a speed of just under a mile per second.

SPACE STATIONS

Space stations are used to carry out studies which cannot be done by satellites or probes. Astronauts may remain on a space station for over a year. Their reactions to life in space help scientists on Earth to understand more about the effects of zero gravity on the human body.

The USA's first space station, Skylab, was launched in 1973. The Russian space station, Mir, was launched in 1986. Specially made pieces, called **modules**, can be attached to or removed from space stations in space. In this way, a station can be adapted according to the mission being carried out on board.

Huge solar panels on the International Space Station will provide it with power.

A joint project of many nations called the **International Space Station (ISS)** should be nearing completion around 2007. Once assembled, it will provide six laboratories for international space research.

THE SPACE SHUTTLE

In the past, satellites and supplies for space stations were launched into space on single-use, unmanned rockets. But this was expensive and inconvenient, as the rockets were mostly made up of fuel tanks, which were jettisoned when empty and could not be re-used.

The USA's **Space Shuttle** was designed as a more efficient alternative. It is boosted into space by two huge, solid-fuel booster rockets. These are released at a height of 28 miles, to be carried slowly down to the sea on parachutes. They can then be retrieved and used again.

At the end of a mission, the Shuttle glides back to Earth. It is protected from the intense heat of re-entry into the atmosphere by special heat-resistant coverings.

The Shuttle's missions usually last about a week. They have included taking astronauts to repair the Hubble Space Telescope*.

See for yourself

At certain times, you can see the ISS, Shuttles and satellites drifting across the sky like slow-moving stars. Various Internet sites tell you when and where to look, and many others have updates on research projects. Some useful Web sites are listed below and on page 29.

Internet links

• Go to **www.usborne-quicklinks.com** for a link to the **StarChild Web site**. Play interactive space games and discover what it's like to be a NASA astronaut – or even how to become one.

• Go to **www.usborne-quicklinks.com** for a link to the **Discovery Web site**. See the gripping story of the first Moon landing, shown in slideshows and movies.

• Go to **www.usborne-quicklinks.com** for a link to **NASA's LIftoff Web site**, to find the exact position in space of the ISS, HST, Space Shuttle and other satellites.

• Go to **www.usborne-quicklinks.com** for a link to the **SEDS Web site**, where you can take a virtual tour of the Space Shuttle, check out its statistics and find answers to questions about it.

*Hubble Space Telescope, 29.

THE EARLY EARTH

The Earth is a tiny planet in a vast universe, which contains billions of stars, planets and moons, as well as huge areas of space containing other, smaller particles. There is no definite proof of how ancient events such as the Earth's formation took place. Many scientists, however, believe that patterns of radiation in space show that the universe was created in a huge explosion about 15 billion years ago. This idea is called the **Big Bang theory**.

Icy comets and rocky asteroids rained down on the Earth's early surface.

BIRTH OF THE EARTH

The Earth is thought to have formed about 4,600 million years ago, and it has been constantly changing and developing ever since. It probably started as a huge, swirling cloud of dust and gases. Over time, this cloud began to shrink and become solid. Heavy iron-rich minerals collected at the middle of the growing planet, eventually creating a core of iron.

As the Earth formed, gases such as methane, hydrogen and ammonia rose from volcanoes on its surface. Over time, ultraviolet radiation from the Sun broke down these poisonous gases, leaving a thick blanket of nitrogen and carbon dioxide. At the same time, steam from volcanoes, and huge chunks of ice which rained down from space, formed early oceans.

This cluster of stars formed many billions of years before the Earth and Sun. Scientists study these ancient stars to try to learn more about the early universe.

EARLY LIFE

Around 3,500 million years ago, simple life-forms developed from the churning chemical soup of the Earth's early oceans. Like modern green plants, they made food using water, carbon dioxide and energy from sunlight. This released oxygen into the early atmosphere.

For many millions of years, these tiny organisms continued to make oxygen from the carbon dioxide surrounding the Earth. This formed a barrier, preventing most of the Sun's harmful ultraviolet rays from reaching the planet. Eventually, conditions were right for complex life-forms to begin their development. For more about life on Earth, see pages 40-41.

ANCIENT HISTORY

The amount of time it has taken the Earth to develop is so vast that it can barely be imagined. For some idea of how ancient the Earth is, try to picture its entire history taking place in one hour. On this scale, each minute would equal about 76.1 million years. Because the history of the Earth goes back so far, scientists must measure its development in periods of millions and billions of years. They use the terms **deep time** or **geological time** to refer to such a vast timescale.

CHANGING CLIMATE

Ever since the Earth began to form, its climate has been changing. For instance, at certain times it was much warmer than it is now. At other times, huge areas were covered with ice.

A glacier forms as snow builds up over many years and becomes a mass of ice. Its huge weight causes it to move slowly downhill.

Ice ages are periods of time lasting for thousands of years, when huge, moving layers of ice called **glaciers** cover much of the Earth. Many scientists think that past ice ages were caused by the Earth's orbit around the Sun changing shape. This would have reduced the amount of sunlight the planet received, leading to an ice age as its climate cooled.

Diagram showing change in Earth's orbit

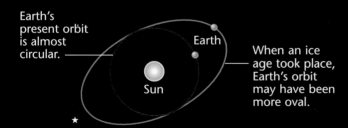

Earth's present orbit is almost circular.

Earth

Sun

When an ice age took place, Earth's orbit may have been more oval.

During an ice age, glaciers travel slowly across the land. In the past, these have helped to shape the landscape in many parts of the world, by carving vast valleys out of rock as they moved. Most of the ice at the North and South Poles may also have been formed during the last ice age.

THE SHAPE OF THE LAND

Soon after the Earth was formed, the first landmasses appeared. They moved around, joined together and split up again many times. About 250 million years ago there was just one giant landmass, called **Pangaea**. It began to split up about 225 million years ago, and the continents which exist today were slowly formed.

Development of modern continents

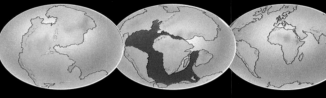

225 million years ago	135 million years ago	Present day

Pangaea

The spreading sea floor (pink area) caused the land to break up.

STUDYING THE PAST

Most of the information scientists have about the Earth's past comes from rocks. Most rocks form in layers over many thousands and millions of years. By studying these layers, scientists called **geologists** can figure out what conditions may have been like as each one was formed.

Rocks formed in warm climates contain more fossils than those formed in cooler climates.

Rocks which were on the Earth's surface during ice ages show signs of being worn away by glaciers.

Internet links

• Go to **www.usborne-quicklinks.com** for a link to the **World Book Web site** to read the fascinating story of Earth's early history.

• Go to **www.usborne-quicklinks.com** for a link to the **Discovery Earth Journeys Web site**. View webcams around the world, take a virtual trip inside the Earth, find out what it would be like to control our planet and keep up to date with the latest geological research.

• Go to **www.usborne-quicklinks.com** for a link to the **Hooper Virtual Natural History Museum Web site** to find out about fossils, extinction, climate change and much more.

• Go to **www.usborne-quicklinks.com** for a link to the **All About Glaciers Web site** where you can read a glacier's life story, and find glacier pictures, news and information.

EARTH'S STRUCTURE

The Earth has a solid surface, but is not solid all the way through. Inside, it is made up of layers, some of which are partly **molten**. This means that they are partly made up of hot liquid. The Earth's middle is an incredibly hot ball of iron and nickel. All the layers are pulled together by the enormous force of gravity from the center.

Diamonds are formed by the tremendous heat and pressure within the Earth's crust.

Cutaway showing the Earth's layers

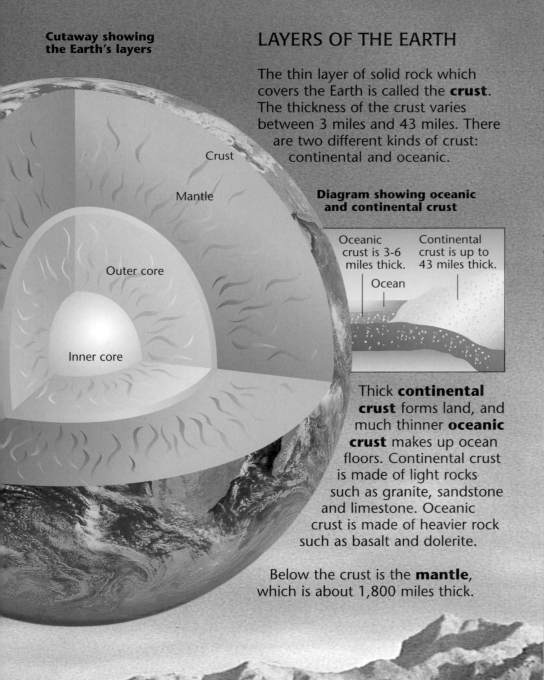

Crust

Mantle

Outer core

Inner core

LAYERS OF THE EARTH

The thin layer of solid rock which covers the Earth is called the **crust**. The thickness of the crust varies between 3 miles and 43 miles. There are two different kinds of crust: continental and oceanic.

Diagram showing oceanic and continental crust

Oceanic crust is 3-6 miles thick.

Continental crust is up to 43 miles thick.

Ocean

Thick **continental crust** forms land, and much thinner **oceanic crust** makes up ocean floors. Continental crust is made of light rocks such as granite, sandstone and limestone. Oceanic crust is made of heavier rock such as basalt and dolerite.

Below the crust is the **mantle**, which is about 1,800 miles thick.

Within the mantle is a thin layer called the **asthenosphere**. This is mostly solid rock, but a small amount is molten rock, called **magma**. This makes the whole layer weak. The upper mantle and crust, together called the **lithosphere**, move around on this weak layer.

The Earth's **core** has two parts. The **outer core**, which is about 1,360 miles thick, is molten. The **inner core** is solid. It is about 780 miles thick, extremely hot (about 9,000°F), and is about the same size as the Moon.

See for yourself

The movement of the liquid outer core is believed to create the Earth's magnetic field. This field creates two poles, called magnetic north and magnetic south. You can see their effects using an ordinary compass. Whichever way you hold the compass, its needle always points to magnetic north.

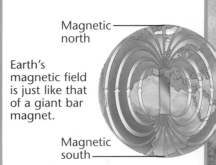

Magnetic north

Earth's magnetic field is just like that of a giant bar magnet.

Magnetic south

PLATES

The lithosphere is divided into large areas called **plates**, which are constantly moving. There are about seven main plates and many smaller ones. Each one is made of continental or oceanic lithosphere, or both. The areas where the plates' edges meet are called **plate boundaries**.

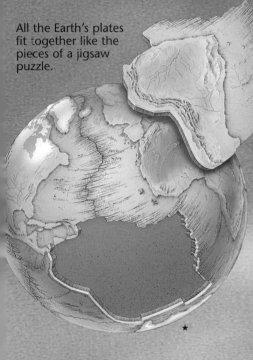

All the Earth's plates fit together like the pieces of a jigsaw puzzle.

The plates move very slowly over the asthenosphere, typically at about 1.5 inches per year. They can move toward each other, move apart or shift sideways.

Because all the plates fit together, movement of one plate affects the others around it. The study of plate movement and its effects is called **plate tectonics**.

NEW FEATURES

Plate movement is constantly causing the formation of new features on the Earth's surface.

For example, where plates move apart below the ocean, magma from the mantle wells up all along the boundary. It cools and hardens to form a mountain range, or **ridge**, of new crust. As the movement continues and more magma wells up along the center, the ridge spreads out sideways, becoming a **spreading ridge**. Boundaries where new crust is formed are called **constructive boundaries**.

A **destructive boundary**, or **subduction zone**, occurs where an oceanic and continental plate move together. The heavier oceanic plate moves beneath the lighter continental plate, forming a **trench** where they meet. As the plate sinks, some of it becomes molten, forming new magma.

Formation of ridges and trenches

Oceanic crust — Trench

Slow currents of hot rock — Ridge

Where two plates push together above ground, the crust buckles and folds upward to form high mountain ranges, called **fold mountains**. The Earth's crust is thickest at these points.

This mountain range was formed by two plates crushing together.

TYPES OF ROCK

The rock that makes up the Earth's surface is constantly being added to. It can be divided into three basic types: igneous, sedimentary and metamorphic.

Igneous rock is formed when molten rock cools and becomes solid. **Sedimentary rock** is formed when sediments, such as rock particles, are deposited by water or weather, buried and then squashed into layers called **strata**. When any type of rock is changed by intense heat or pressure, **metamorphic rock** is formed.

Granite is a type of igneous rock.

Limestone is a type of sedimentary rock.

Marble is a type of metamorphic rock.

Internet links

• Go to **www.usborne-quicklinks.com** for a link to the **BBC Web site** to find out about the three main rock types, conduct rock experiments at home and see an animation of the Earth's rocky past.

• Go to **www.usborne-quicklinks.com** for a link to the **Savage Earth Web site**, where you can read essays about the Earth's structure, its volcanoes, earthquakes and gigantic ocean waves. Richly illustrated with movies, animations and images.

• Go to **www.usborne-quicklinks.com** for a link to the **PBS Mountain Maker, Earth Shaker Web site** to pull and push virtual tectonic plates and see what happens to the Earth. This site provides a useful introduction to plate tectonics.

FAULTS

As plates move, the strain sometimes causes brittle rock to crack. These cracks, called **faults**, are often weak zones where more movement or cracking may occur. For example, **rift valleys** may form when land containing faults is forced in opposite directions. All plate boundaries are major faults which began as minor ones.

Formation of a rift valley

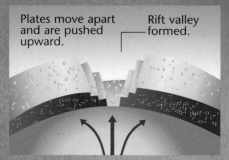

Plates move apart and are pushed upward.

Rift valley formed.

Rock is pushed upward from underneath and pulled apart at faults.

EARTHQUAKES

The constant movement of plates causes pressure to build up at faults, and at the plate boundaries themselves. If there is a sudden slippage of rock, this pressure is released quickly, and an **earthquake** occurs. Most earthquakes are too weak to be felt by people, but some cause huge damage, as the ground shakes and buildings collapse.

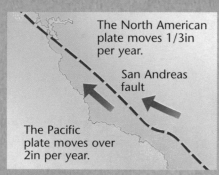

The North American plate moves 1/3in per year.

San Andreas fault

The Pacific plate moves over 2in per year.

Earthquakes often occur on the San Andreas fault, on America's west coast. This is because the two plates on either side of the fault slide in the same direction at different speeds.

FOCUS

The point where energy is suddenly released and an earthquake starts is called the **focus**. It is usually 3-9 miles under the ground. The point on the surface directly above the focus is called the **epicenter**. Vibrations called **seismic waves** travel from the focus in all directions.

An earthquake is caused when rock gives way at a fault, releasing vast amounts of built-up energy.

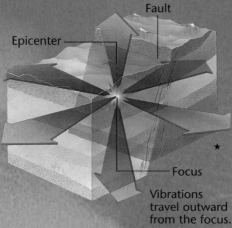

Fault

Epicenter

Focus

Vibrations travel outward from the focus.

PREDICTION

Scientists who study earthquakes, called **seismologists**, use plate movement to predict when major earthquakes are going to happen. Horizontal movement along plates can be measured by bouncing a laser beam off a series of reflectors on the ground. A computer records the time it takes to travel between them. If this changes, it shows that ground movement has taken place. Animal behavior may also be used to predict an earthquake.

Snakes came out of hibernation early before an earthquake in China in 1975. This may have been because they were disturbed by very slight vibrations in the ground.

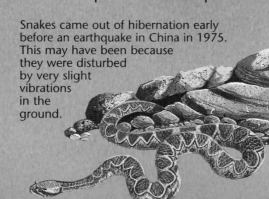

VOLCANOES

The magma within the largely solid mantle sometimes rises and collects in certain places. **Volcanoes** are formed when it rises to the Earth's surface and bursts out. At this stage magma becomes known as **lava**. This explosive effect is known as an **eruption**. Most volcanoes form along plate boundaries or under the sea.

Inside an erupting volcano

The volcano below, called a **composite volcano**, is made up of alternating layers of lava and ash. These have built up over long periods of time to form a steep-sided cone.

1. Place where magma gathers beneath Earth's crust, called **magma chamber**
2. **Vent** – the main pipe up the middle of a volcano
3. **Dyke** – a magma-filled channel from the vent to the surface
4. Layers of ash and lava
5. Hole at top of volcano, called a **crater**
6. Dust, ash and gases
7. Lumps of lava, called **volcanic bombs**

VOLCANO FORMATION

A row of volcanoes may form where plates are moving apart, particularly at spreading ridges*.

Spreading ridges form when plates move apart.

Volcanoes may also form above subduction zones*, where one plate is forced beneath the other.

At subduction zones, one plate is forced below the other plate, where it starts to melt.

Some volcanoes form in the middle of plates, at hot patches on the Earth's surface called **hot spots**. Scientists think that these are formed when especially hot currents of magma called **plumes** shoot up and burn through the crust, bursting out of the surface.

DEAD OR ALIVE?

Volcanoes that erupt regularly are known as **active** volcanoes. If it is thought that a volcano will never erupt again, it is said to be **extinct**. Sometimes, people think a volcano has become extinct, but it is actually just inactive, or **dormant**.

SUPERVOLCANOES

Supervolcanoes are formed from huge collapsed craters, called **calderas**, with a magma chamber beneath. Only a few supervolcanoes exist, but they are so powerful and destructive that a single eruption could alter all life on Earth. This is because enormous pressure builds up in the magma chamber over thousands of years, then bursts in a devastating explosion.

Scientists think that the last supervolcano eruption was in Sumatra, 74,000 years ago. It is believed that this eruption blew out enough ash to block the Sun's light for around six months, causing the Earth to cool down. This would have caused environmental changes all over the world, killing huge numbers of living things.

Here, fountains of lava are shooting out of an erupting volcano. They may travel up to 2,000 feet into the air.

See for yourself

You can do a simple test to show how seismic waves travel from an earthquake focus. Place a handful of sand or grit on a table, then tap the table gently with a hammer. This point is the "focus", and the waves which travel outwards will make the sand jump. Try striking the table further from the sand, and see what happens. The waves lose strength as they travel further away from the focus.

Internet links

- Go to **www.usborne-quicklinks.com** for a link to the **BrainPop Web site** to watch a movie about plate tectonics.

- Go to **www.usborne-quicklinks.com** for a link to the **Great Quakes Web site** for amazing earthquake images, activities and animations.

- Go to **www.usborne-quicklinks.com** for a link to the **Volcano World Web site**, where you can explore dozens of different volcanoes around the world.

- Go to **www.usborne-quicklinks.com** for a link to the **Volcanoes Online Web site** to read about plate tectonics, search a volcano database and play volcano games.

- Go to **www.usborne-quicklinks.com** for links to the **U.S. Geological Survey Web site** to find a useful introduction to earthquakes, or examine an online plate tectonics textbook.

THE ATMOSPHERE

The Earth is surrounded by a blanket of different gases called the **atmosphere**. It is the presence of this atmosphere that allows life on Earth to exist, as it contains oxygen and other gases needed by living things. The atmosphere also acts as a shield against harmful ultraviolet rays from the Sun.

The atmosphere protects our planet from the Sun's powerful rays.

EARLY FORMATION

When the Earth was forming, it was first surrounded by hydrogen and helium. However, as the Sun heated these light gases, they escaped into space.

An atmosphere which could be held in place by the Earth's gravity was eventually formed from gases such as methane, ammonia and water vapor. These poured out of volcanoes on the surface, in a process known as **outgassing**. Over billions of years, these gases reacted to form an atmosphere of nitrogen and carbon dioxide.

Earth's early atmosphere would have been poisonous to living things. It took millions of years to become the way it is today.

The atmosphere as we know it did not start to form until plant-like organisms appeared in Earth's oceans, around 3,500 million years ago. These very simple living things used the Sun's light to make food from water and carbon dioxide, releasing oxygen as a by-product. This process continued for many millions of years, until there was enough oxygen in the atmosphere to support other forms of life.

These single-celled cyanobacteria were among the first organisms on Earth.

OUR ATMOSPHERE

The atmosphere is a mixture of gases – around four-fifths nitrogen and one-fifth oxygen, with traces of others. Water also exists in the atmosphere as vapor, droplets in clouds, and as ice crystals.

Snowflakes are formed from ice crystals.

Percentage of gases in the atmosphere

Nitrogen	78%
Oxygen	21%
Argon	0.9%
Carbon dioxide	0.03%
Other gases (such as xenon, neon, krypton)	0.07%

ATMOSPHERIC LAYERS

The atmosphere is around 310 miles thick and is made up of several layers. These extend out from the Earth and fade into space. All the Earth's weather happens in the layer nearest the surface. Most of the higher atmosphere is a thin mix of calm, unchanging gases.

Layers in the atmosphere, showing number of miles from Earth

Exosphere (over 310 miles)

The atmosphere merges into space. This layer contains almost no gases.

Thermosphere (up to 310 miles)

Temperature in this layer is very high, because of a gas called atomic oxygen. This helps to absorb some radiation from the Sun.

The Space Shuttle orbits in the thermosphere.

Mesosphere (up to 50 miles)

This layer has no ozone and no clouds, so the temperature is low.

Meteors burn up here.

Stratosphere (up to 30 miles)

This layer contains about 19% of all the atmosphere's gases. Temperature is higher, because it contains the ozone layer (see right).

Jet planes fly in the stratosphere.

Troposphere (up to 6 miles)

Contains 80% of all gases in the atmosphere, as well as all weather. Temperature in this layer decreases with height.

CHANGING ATMOSPHERE

Burning fuels and forests has released extra carbon dioxide into the atmosphere. Plants can't convert this to oxygen quickly enough, so the carbon dioxide has built up, trapping the Sun's heat around the Earth. This **greenhouse effect** is likely to cause **global warming**, a rise in future global temperatures.

Smoke from burning fuels adds carbon dioxide to the atmosphere.

The Sun's rays, absorbed and given back out by the Earth, are trapped by the carbon dioxide and sent back down.

People have already begun to take steps to reduce the release of gases that lead to global warming. The main way that this can be done is by using alternative energy sources, such as wind or solar power.

This mountaineer has to carry a supply of oxygen, because the air in the troposphere contains less oxygen as he climbs higher.

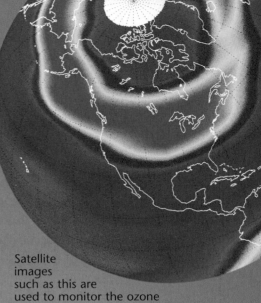

Satellite images such as this are used to monitor the ozone layer. Orange areas show where ozone levels are highest.

THE OZONE LAYER

Within the stratosphere is a layer of **ozone** gas. This absorbs most of the Sun's harmful ultraviolet radiation, preventing it from reaching the Earth.

The ozone layer is being damaged by man-made gases called **chlorofluorocarbons (CFCs)**. These are released by some refrigerators and aerosols, and react with sunlight in the stratosphere. The products of this reaction break down the ozone. As the layer becomes thinner, more ultraviolet rays reach the Earth's surface.

Internet links

• Go to **www.usborne-quicklinks.com** for a link to the **Kapili Web site** to find a friendly introduction to the atmosphere.

• Go to **www.usborne-quicklinks.com** for links to the **ARM (Atmospheric Radiation Monitoring Project) Web site** for useful global warming resourses.

• Go to **www.usborne-quicklinks.com** for a link to **NASA's TOMS (Total Ozone Mapping Spectrometer) Web site** to investigate the ozone layer and atmosphere using images taken from space.

• Go to **www.usborne-quicklinks.com** for a link to the **BBC Science in Action Web site**. Discover the power of air through scientific investigations using drinking straws, fires and creamcakes.

LIFE ON EARTH

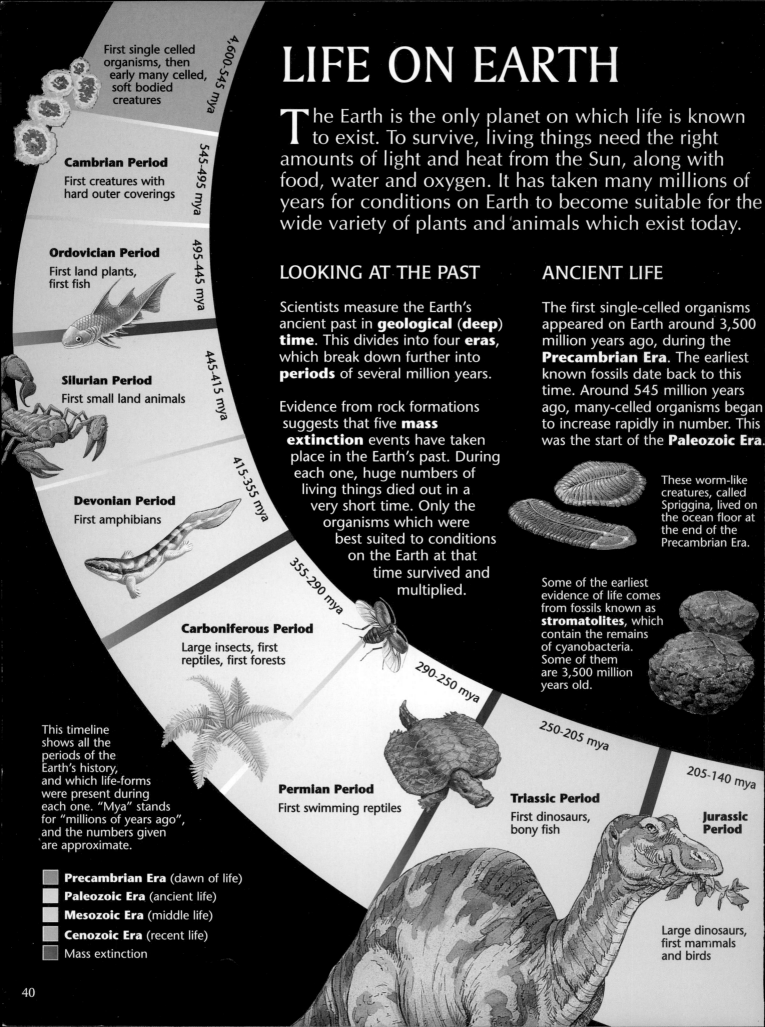

The Earth is the only planet on which life is known to exist. To survive, living things need the right amounts of light and heat from the Sun, along with food, water and oxygen. It has taken many millions of years for conditions on Earth to become suitable for the wide variety of plants and animals which exist today.

LOOKING AT THE PAST

Scientists measure the Earth's ancient past in **geological (deep) time**. This divides into four **eras**, which break down further into **periods** of several million years.

Evidence from rock formations suggests that five **mass extinction** events have taken place in the Earth's past. During each one, huge numbers of living things died out in a very short time. Only the organisms which were best suited to conditions on the Earth at that time survived and multiplied.

ANCIENT LIFE

The first single-celled organisms appeared on Earth around 3,500 million years ago, during the **Precambrian Era**. The earliest known fossils date back to this time. Around 545 million years ago, many-celled organisms began to increase rapidly in number. This was the start of the **Paleozoic Era**.

These worm-like creatures, called Spriggina, lived on the ocean floor at the end of the Precambrian Era.

Some of the earliest evidence of life comes from fossils known as **stromatolites**, which contain the remains of cyanobacteria. Some of them are 3,500 million years old.

First single celled organisms, then early many celled, soft bodied creatures

4,600-545 mya

Cambrian Period
First creatures with hard outer coverings

545-495 mya

Ordovician Period
First land plants, first fish

495-445 mya

Silurian Period
First small land animals

445-415 mya

Devonian Period
First amphibians

415-355 mya

355-290 mya

Carboniferous Period
Large insects, first reptiles, first forests

290-250 mya

250-205 mya

205-140 mya

This timeline shows all the periods of the Earth's history, and which life-forms were present during each one. "Mya" stands for "millions of years ago", and the numbers given are approximate.

Permian Period
First swimming reptiles

Triassic Period
First dinosaurs, bony fish

Jurassic Period

Large dinosaurs, first mammals and birds

- **Precambrian Era** (dawn of life)
- **Paleozoic Era** (ancient life)
- **Mesozoic Era** (middle life)
- **Cenozoic Era** (recent life)
- Mass extinction

DEVELOPING LIFE

Fossil records suggest that in a part of the Paleozoic Era called the **Cambrian Period**, there was a huge increase in the number of different creatures on the Earth. Sea creatures began to develop hard body parts. These protective coverings would have made the creatures tougher, increasing their chances of living long enough to reproduce.

Many creatures with hard body coverings, like this trilobite, began to appear in seas during the Cambrian Period.

Some small arthropods (creatures with jointed bodies), such as millipedes and insects, were able to move onto the land. This was because the Earth's temperature had cooled enough for land plants to grow in large numbers, providing food. The earliest vertebrates (animals with backbones) also appeared.

During the **Devonian Period** (around 415-355 million years ago), the climate in many areas was hot and dry, and water levels dropped in rivers and lakes. One group of fish became able to breathe both in and out of water. These were the earliest amphibians.

This fossil shows that seed-carrying plants existed in the Devonian Period.

Around 355 million years ago, during the **Carboniferous Period**, many parts of the world became hot and humid. This allowed huge numbers of plants to grow, forming vast, steamy swamps. These became home to many types of bugs and amphibians.

Meganeura, a giant dragonfly, had wings that measured 60cm across.

THE AGE OF REPTILES

During the **Permian Period**, amphibians evolved into early reptiles. They were able to spread all over the world because all the land became joined together as one huge continent. At the same time, huge numbers of sea creatures died because the shallow seas around the continents disappeared.

Hylonomus was one of the earliest known reptiles.

The **Mesozoic Era** began 250 million years ago, with numbers of reptiles increasing rapidly. During this era, the dinosaurs appeared. They became the dominant vertebrate life-forms on the Earth until 65 million years ago, when they suddenly died out, probably as a result of a major climatic change.

THE AGE OF MAMMALS

The current age of mammals, called the **Cenozoic Era**, began after the dinosaurs died out. It is thought that mammals may have survived the change in climate which killed the dinosaurs because they can control their own body temperature. Dinosaurs probably could not do this.

MODERN EXTINCTION

Extinction has always happened naturally over time. However, the current extinction rate is thought to be about 10,000 times greater than it would be if humans did not exist. Modern extinctions are almost always caused by pollution or loss of habitats (natural living spaces), brought about by the growing human race, and its need for land, food and water.

The white rhino is one of many species threatened by habitat loss or hunting.

Unless we can make better use of the Earth's resources, it is possible that humans may be responsible for the next major extinction event.

1.8 mya to present day

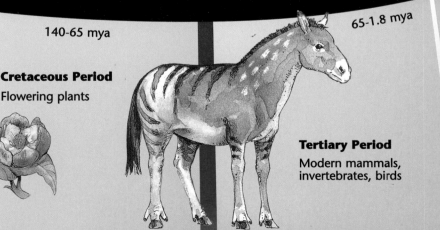

140-65 mya

Cretaceous Period
Flowering plants

65-1.8 mya

Tertiary Period
Modern mammals, invertebrates, birds

Quaternary Period
Appearance of humans

Internet links

• Go to **www.usborne-quicklinks.com** for a link to the **Museum of Paleantology Web site**, where you can explore Earth's history, era by era.

• Go to **www.usborne-quicklinks.com** for a link to the **Discovering Dinosaurs Web site** to try some dinosaur activities.

SEAS AND OCEANS

Around 71% of the Earth's surface is covered in salty water, which makes up five vast oceans and several smaller seas. Oceans are very important to life on Earth, and are home to huge numbers of living things. The oceans also influence weather and climate conditions all over the world.

OCEAN CURRENTS

Ocean water constantly moves in huge, flowing bands called **currents**. These carry vast amounts of water around the Earth. There are two main types of ocean currents: surface and deep. **Surface currents** affect the top 380yds or so of oceans. They are pushed along by **prevailing winds** (the most common types of wind in an area).

Deep currents are made up of very cold water coming from the North and South Poles. Cold water is heavier, so it sinks beneath the warmer surface currents which constantly arrive at the Poles. It then drifts toward the equator, where it warms up and rises to become a surface current itself. It then changes direction and starts to drift back toward the Poles.

How currents circulate

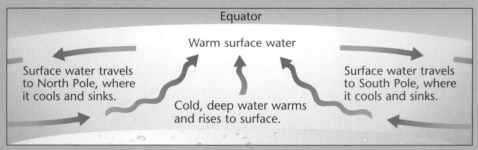

Equator

Warm surface water

Surface water travels to North Pole, where it cools and sinks.

Cold, deep water warms and rises to surface.

Surface water travels to South Pole, where it cools and sinks.

Pacific Ocean

The largest of Earth's vast oceans, called the Pacific, covers around 30% of the planet's surface.

See for yourself

You can do a simple activity to show that cold water is heavier than warmer water. Half fill a large, clear bowl with warm water. Fill a jug with ice-cold water containing a little food coloring. Gently pour the water into the bowl. You should notice that it sinks, just as cold water does at the Poles.

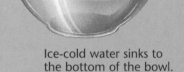

Ice-cold water sinks to the bottom of the bowl.

CLIMATE CONTROL

Oceans and seas play an important role in controlling the world's climate. Their waters absorb heat from the Sun, especially in tropical regions, and spread it around the Earth in surface currents.

Warm ocean currents may cause **tropical cyclones** (called **hurricanes** in America and **typhoons** in the Far East). These are fierce storms, with strong winds which form waves up to 27yds high.

How a tropical cyclone forms

Moist, warm air above the ocean rises and cools, forming clouds.

Air from the surrounding ocean surface rushes into the space and begins to spiral upward.

Wind speeds increase; and land in the cyclone's path is hit by a fierce storm.

TIDAL MOVEMENT

Seas and oceans are constantly moved by the tides. Tidal movement is caused mainly by the Moon. As it travels around the Earth, the force of its gravity makes the water on either side of the Earth bulge out. In a 24-hour period, this causes two **high tides**, when sea levels are at their highest, and two **low tides**, when they are at their lowest.

Tides are also influenced by the Earth, Moon and Sun lining up in certain ways. At full moon and new moon, there are very high **spring tides**. At quarters, when the Moon and Sun are at right angles to each other, there are very low **neap tides**.

Spring tide

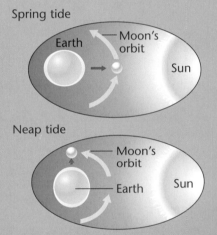

Earth — Moon's orbit

Sun

Neap tide

Moon's orbit

Earth

Sun

LIFE IN THE OCEANS

Seas and oceans contain a huge variety of plant and animal life, from the surface all the way down to the deepest trenches. Billions of microscopic plants called **phytoplankton** drift near the surface of the water. These are the main source of food for many creatures which live and feed at different ocean levels, called **zones**.

Ocean feeding zones

Sea level

Tuna

The **sunlit zone** is home to all the plants and many animals.

220yds

Swordfish

In the **twilight zone**, only a little light gets through.

1,095yds

Lantern fish

The **sunless zone** is very cold. Animals feed mainly on dead plankton which sink from the surface.

4,375yds

The **abyssal zone** is freezing and dark. Many animals in this zone can produce light from their bodies.

Angler fish

5,500yds

Crinoid (sea lily)

Animals in ocean trenches may be almost 4 miles from the surface.

Internet links

• Go to **www.usborne-quicklinks.com** for a link to the **Sea and Sky Web site** for news, games and lots to explore.

• Go to **www.usborne-quicklinks.com** for a link to the **Ocean Planet Web site**, a fascinating ocean exhibition.

• Go to **www.usborne-quicklinks.com** for a link to the **PBS Savage Seas Web site** to study waves, weather and survival.

• Go to **www.usborne-quicklinks.com** for a link to the **Franklin Institute Web site** to find out about El Niño.

• Go to **www.usborne-quicklinks.com** for a link to the **Voyage to the Deep Web site** to explore the ocean in a deep-sea sub.

• Go to **www.usborne-quicklinks.com** for a link to the **Oceanlink Web site** for lots of good marine science information.

RIVERS

Rivers are formed when small streams join together and flow across the land, eventually flowing into a sea or lake. Rivers shape the Earth's surface by wearing away the rock they flow over and depositing rocks, pebbles, sand and silt as they do so.

A RIVER'S SOURCE

The beginning of a river is called its **source**. Many rivers have their source in mountain regions where water has run across the surface from various places and flowed into one channel. A river may also begin as a spring or a flow from a glacier.

How springs are formed

Rain or snow falls on **permeable** rock, which lets in water.

Water soaks into rock, building up from the lowest permeable level.

Springs begin to flow where the water-filled rock meets the surface.

A waterfall forms when a river flows from hard to soft rock. The water wears away the soft rock more quickly and forms a ledge.

STAGES OF A RIVER

A river's course can be divided into three stages. In its **upper** stage, the valley tends to be V-shaped with steep sides, formed as the turbulent water cuts down into the rock. The slope or **gradient** of the river's rocky bed is steep.

In the **middle** stage, the river's speed increases because the bed is smoother. The gradient is more gentle, and the valley becomes wider as the water wears away its sides. The river flows from side to side in wide loops. This is called **meandering**.

In the **lower** stage, the river's muddy or sandy bed is even smoother, so it flows faster. The river is large, because it has been joined by others, called **tributaries**. At its end it flows into the sea or a lake.

Each wide loop is called a **meander**.

The wide, flat valley floor is called the **flood plain**.

The river has split into several channels. This area is called a delta.

Lower stage

Middle stage

Upper stage

V-shaped valley

EROSION

Running water wears away or **erodes** rock by the constant movement of the pebbles and sand grains it carries. This is how a river bed forms. The amount of erosion depends on the speed and amount of water, how much material it carries and the rock it flows over. Softer rock, such as sandstone, is eroded faster than harder rock, such as granite.

The diagram below shows four types of erosion which take place at different stages of a river's course. The length of the river is not shown to scale.

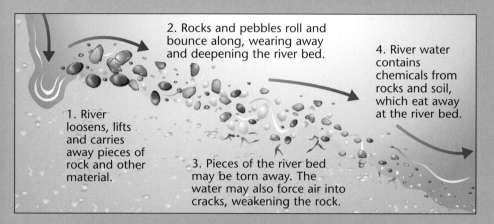

2. Rocks and pebbles roll and bounce along, wearing away and deepening the river bed.

4. River water contains chemicals from rocks and soil, which eat away at the river bed.

1. River loosens, lifts and carries away pieces of rock and other material.

3. Pieces of the river bed may be torn away. The water may also force air into cracks, weakening the rock.

TRANSPORTATION

All the material **transported**, or carried along, by a river is called its **load**. Finer particles of clay and silt are carried along with heavier ones, such as pebbles and boulders. Wherever a river slows down, some of this material is deposited. The heaviest material is deposited first, followed by the smaller particles, creating a layering effect.

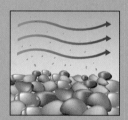

Large particles sink to the river bed before smaller ones.

DELTAS

As a river flows into the sea, any material it is still carrying is deposited. If this is deposited faster than it is washed away by the sea's currents and tides, it builds up in an area of flat land called a **delta**. The river splits into narrower channels as it crosses the delta and travels to the sea, creating a number of **sediment islands**. As the fresh river water and the salty sea water meet, chemical reactions take place and minerals that have been carried down, dissolved in the fresh water, come out of solution and are added to the sediment.

This is a delta in the Tenakee Inlet, Alaska. You can see how the sediment has built up in islands.

The mineral-rich sediment in delta areas makes the land fertile and ideal for farming. In Bangladesh, for example, millions of people live on islands formed in the delta of the River Ganges, despite the threat of flooding.

See for yourself

You can show how water deposits materials in layers. First, cut two 1 inch slits in the bottom of a 2 liter plastic bottle. Cover each slit with tape.

Tape over slits.

Next, use a funnel to half fill the bottle with soil. Then almost fill the bottle with water. Screw on the lid, shake vigorously, and leave for 24 hours.

Plastic tubing

Remove the lid and place one end of some plastic tubing in the water. Suck the water up, making sure not to swallow any, then put your thumb over the end. Bend the tube downward into the sink or a container. Move your thumb, and the water will drain out.

Finally, pull the tape off the slits in the base, and leave to drain for 24 hours. You should see the soil has settled in layers.

Bottle cut away

Internet links

• Go to **www.usborne-quicklinks.com** for a link to the **Rivers and Streams Web site** for useful information.

• Go to **www.usborne-quicklinks.com** for a link to the **Watershed Game Web site** where you can play a watershed game and discover the importance of fresh water.

• Go to **www.usborne-quicklinks.com** for a link to the **US Geological Survey's Water Web site** for images and games.

• Go to **www.usborne-quicklinks.com** for a link to the **Environment Canada Web site** to learn about groundwater in Canada, and why it is a precious resource.

• Go to **www.usborne-quicklinks.com** for a link to the **Fundamentals of Physical Geography Web site**, for advanced information about erosion.

WEATHER

The conditions in the atmosphere near to the Earth's surface are called the **weather**. These conditions include the temperature of the air, wind speed, air pressure, and the amount of water in the air, called **humidity**. Other factors include the amount of cloud and how much rain or snow falls, called **precipitation**.

THE SUN'S EFFECT

The Sun plays the most important part in causing the weather. Its heat, known as **solar radiation**, is absorbed by the Earth, which warms up as a result. In turn, the heat passes out from the Earth to the air above, which also becomes warmer.

The Sun's rays have the strongest effect where they hit the Earth's surface straight on, that is, around the middle of the Earth (the **equator**). Further away from the equator, the rays do not strike directly, so the heat is spread over a larger area. Its effect is therefore weaker.

How the Sun's rays strike the Earth

AIR PRESSURE

The atmosphere presses down on the Earth's surface, creating **atmospheric pressure**. When air is heated from below, it expands and begins to rise. As it does so it stops pressing down so hard on the surface. This creates an area of **low pressure**. At the surface, air flows in from surrounding areas to even up the pressure.

Low pressure

As warm air rises from the surface, more air moves in from higher pressure areas.

High pressure

As cooler air pushes down, the surface air moves away to lower pressure areas.

Around the Earth there are areas of high and low pressure. These areas are called **belts**. Strong winds blow from high pressure belts to low pressure belts. However, the winds do not just blow straight from one belt to the other. They are deflected sideways (made to swerve) by the Earth's rotation. This is known as the **Coriolis effect**.

Red arrows show how winds are deflected around the Earth. Yellow arrow shows which way the Earth rotates.

HOT AND COLD AIR

As warm air rises, it cools and sinks back to Earth. There, it may be heated again if the surface is still warmer than the air above. The circulation of warm and cold currents of air is called **convection** and the currents are **convection currents**.

Rising current of warm air

Warm air eventually cools and sinks.

Surrounding cooler air moves in to replace warm air.

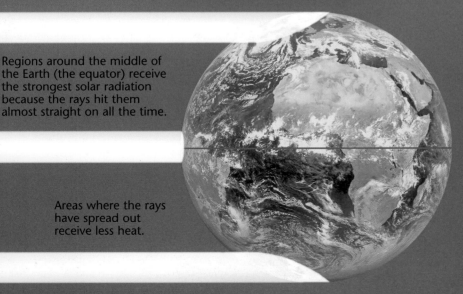

Regions around the middle of the Earth (the equator) receive the strongest solar radiation because the rays hit them almost straight on all the time.

Areas where the rays have spread out receive less heat.

These dark clouds are full of water droplets, which may fall as rain, snow or hail.

CLOUDS

The Sun's heat causes water to evaporate from the seas. The water vapor rises and cools, condensing as it does so, to form tiny water droplets. These mass together as **clouds**. When clouds form slowly and steadily, they spread out across the sky in sheets. On hot days, they grow faster and puff up into heaps.

Common types of cloud

Cirrus clouds are high and wispy.

Cumulus clouds often form high in the sky in warm, sunny weather.

Stratus clouds form low, flat layers.

THE SEASONS

Weather conditions change throughout the year. These changes are called the **seasons**, and they occur because the Earth is tilted at an angle in relation to the Sun. As the planet makes its year-long journey around the Sun, the most direct sunlight falls on different areas.

In January, at the start of each orbit, the **southern hemisphere** (the half of the Earth below the equator) is tilted toward the Sun, causing temperatures to rise there. In June, the **northern hemisphere** is tilted toward the Sun. Temperatures rise in the north and fall in the south. In spring and fall, neither hemisphere is tilted more toward the Sun.

Diagram showing how seasons change

In June, the northern hemisphere is warmer.

In March, neither hemisphere is warmed more.

Equator

Sun's rays

In September, neither hemisphere is warmed more than the other.

In January, the southern hemisphere is warmest.

See for yourself

You can do this simple activity to create a miniature cloud. First, fill a large, clear plastic container about a third full with hot water. Next, place some ice cubes on a baking tray and put this on top of the container. As the air inside the container rises and is cooled by the ice, the water vapor it contains forms droplets, making a small "cloud".

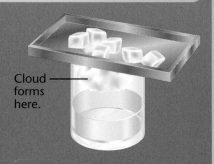

Cloud forms here.

Internet links

• Go to **www.usborne-quicklinks.com** for a link to the **Windows to the World Web site,** where you can find out what causes the seasons.

• Go to **www.usborne-quicklinks.com** for a link to the **Meteorology Guide Web site** to learn about many different types of weather.

• Go to **www.usborne-quicklinks.com** for a link to the **PSC Weather Center Cloud Boutique Web site** to find detailed cloud information and images.

CLIMATE

An area's **climate** is its typical pattern of weather conditions and temperature over a long period of time. One type of climate may affect a large region, or a small, local area, where it is called a **microclimate**. Climates depend on latitude, distance from the sea, and height above sea level.

Banana trees such as this grow in equatorial areas.

CLIMATIC REGIONS

A **climatic region** is a large area on the Earth within which the climate is generally the same. The world's major climatic regions are described on this page.

Polar climates are harsh and change very little throughout the year. The temperature is extremely low and there is little rain or snowfall. Hardly any plant life can grow in these conditions.

Many polar animals, such as this polar bear, are kept warm by a thick layer of fur or fat.

Tundra regions have harsh winds and low winter temperatures, averaging from -22°F to -4°F. The temperature rises to around 62°F during the summer.

Tough, low-growing land plants such as lichens are examples of tundra vegetation.

In **temperate** regions, rain falls throughout the year, and the temperature varies with the seasons. It is generally between 21°F and 77°F. Day-to-day weather changes are a feature of temperate regions.

Deciduous trees, which lose their leaves in the fall, are found in temperate areas.

Tropical regions have a warm climate all year round. There are two seasons, dry and wet. Temperatures tend to be between 70°F and 86°F.

Grasslands in tropical regions are mostly made up of scattered trees and tall grasses, which die off in the dry season.

Mediterranean areas are warm and wet in winter but dry in summer. Their climate is heavily influenced by currents of air which move between the land and sea.

Citrus fruits grow well in Mediterranean climates. Their thick skins prevent them from drying up during the hot summer months.

Continental areas, such as the central parts of Asia and North America, have hot summers and cold winters.

North American prairies have very hot summers.

Equatorial regions have a constantly hot and wet climate, which supports rainforests in many areas. The temperature never drops below around 63°F, creating ideal growing conditions for huge numbers of plants.

Desert climates are generally very dry, with less than 9.8 inches of rainfall per year. Daytime temperatures in the hottest deserts may be over 100°F, although some become much cooler in winter. Many living things in the desert can store water.

Cacti and many other desert plants store large amounts of water in their thick, fleshy leaves.

MOUNTAIN CLIMATES

In mountain areas, temperatures drop as height above sea level (**altitude**) increases, producing different climates and vegetation at different altitudes. Trees can't survive on high mountain slopes because there is little soil, and the ground may be frozen and blasted by harsh, icy winds.

The direction which a mountainside faces (called its **aspect**) also affects its climate. If one side of a mountain receives more sunlight than the other, more vegetation may grow there.

Plant life in a mountain climate

Small, low-growing plants such as moss and lichens grow on the high mountainside.

Above a certain level, called the **treeline**, it is too cold for trees to grow.

Trees

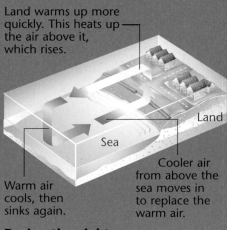

COASTAL CLIMATES

In coastal areas, the land and sea gain and lose heat at different rates during the day and night. The air above them constantly circulates, creating a mild, wet climate. This is known as a **coastal** or **maritime** climate.

During the day

Land warms up more quickly. This heats up the air above it, which rises.

Land

Sea

Warm air cools, then sinks again.

Cooler air from above the sea moves in to replace the warm air.

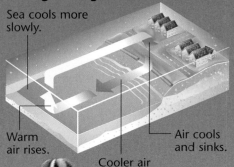

During the night

Sea cools more slowly.

Warm air rises.

Cooler air moves out.

Air cools and sinks.

CITY CLIMATES

Cities tend to be warmer than the areas surrounding them. This is because concrete absorbs more heat than vegetation. It also holds on to heat for longer, making nights warmer in cities than in the countryside.

The ground beneath a city also tends to be drier, as roads and pavements prevent water from draining into the soil beneath.

See for yourself

This simple test shows how plants from different climatic regions lose water. First, water a potted geranium and a cactus, then place a plastic bag around each of their pots. Stand them on plates. Next, cut the bases off two large plastic bottles. Smear petroleum jelly on the bottom of each one, and put them over the plants.

Bottle (lid on)

Bag (tied at base of plant)

After three days, you should see water droplets in the bottles. The cactus comes from hot areas where water is scarce, so it will have given out much less than the geranium.

Internet links

- Go to **www.usborne-quicklinks.com** for a link to the **On the Line Web site**, for desert climate information.

- Go to **www.usborne-quicklinks.com** for a link to the **Build-a-Prairie Web site** to build your own virtual prairie.

- Go to **www.usborne-quicklinks.com** for a link to the **National Geographic Web site**, where you can visit an online climate laboratory.

- Go to **www.usborne-quicklinks.com** for a link to the **Fundamentals of Physical Geography Web site** to learn about the different climatic regions.

- Go to **www.usborne-quicklinks.com** for a link to **the Living Africa Web site** to discover the amazing Sahara desert.

WORLD POPULATION

All the people living in a particular place are called its **population**. Today, the world's population is greater than ever before, and it is increasing all the time. People's need for food, shelter and fuel creates demands on the Earth and its resources. As a result, people have altered the natural environment to suit their needs.

Hong Kong is so overcrowded that thousands of people live on boats in the harbor.

SPREADING OUT

If all the Earth's surface were suitable to live on, there would be plenty of room for everyone. However, few people live where the climate is very hot or cold, or where the soil is unsuitable for farming. This means that the world's population is spread unevenly over the continents.

There are now over 6 billion people in the world, compared to around 4 billion in 1980. In countries with fast-growing populations, more people are being forced to live in overcrowded conditions or unsuitable places.

This satellite image shows Washington DC, USA. Over a third of the world's population lives in cities like this.

Graph showing world population since the year 1000

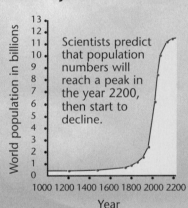

Scientists predict that population numbers will reach a peak in the year 2200, then start to decline.

World population in billions

Year

CITY PROBLEMS

All over the world, people move from the country into towns and cities, to find work. This is called **urban migration**. As city populations grow, some areas become crowded, and pollution increases.

In some countries, **shanty towns**, made up of makeshift buildings, build up on the edges of cities to house the extra people. Houses in shanty towns are usually built from waste materials and scrap. There is often no clean water supply, electricity or sewage system.

This is a shanty town on the outskirts of Cape Town, South Africa. People may be forced to build these when they can't afford housing in the city, or when there isn't enough available.

POPULATION CONTROL

Many countries are trying to prevent their population from growing too quickly. For example, in China, couples are discouraged from having more than one child. Health education projects also teach people **birth control** – how to avoid having too many children. However, many people object to birth control because of their religious or cultural beliefs.

PEOPLE AND THE LAND

Since early times, people's lives have been influenced by the natural features of their surroundings. People looked for areas where they could find water, food and safety from attack. When they discovered a suitable place, they formed permanent groups called **communities**.

Many communities began near rivers, springs or wells, or in areas that were not likely to flood. Fertile soils for farming and natural resources, such as coal, also encouraged people to settle in particular places.

EFFECTS ON THE LAND

People often change their surroundings to suit their needs. Over the centuries, more and more land has been cleared for building, transportation systems and growing crops. Huge areas of forests have been destroyed and natural wetlands drained. Dry areas have been watered artificially or **irrigated**.

Here, a wooded area is being cleared to make way for a building site.

These methods help to provide more food, housing, and transport routes. But the natural world suffers as a result. In many areas of cleared land, fertile topsoil has been washed or blown away. This is called **soil erosion**. It leaves infertile soil, which cannot be used to grow crops. In some countries, soil erosion combined with drought has led to famine.

FARMING

As the world's population increases, so does the demand for food. Many international charities are helping to improve farming techniques in developing countries. They set up projects to teach farmers how to produce more crops from the same amount of land. This removes the need to clear more land.

Some new farmland has been created in desert border land. These areas once had trees and shrubs, but have been turned to desert through soil erosion. This is caused by overgrazing, tree felling and dry winds. But with the help of irrigation, this land may be used to grow crops.

In areas with very little water, drip irrigators deliver water drop by drop to each plant. Sometimes fertilizers are added to the water. This is known as **fertigation**.

Internet links

• Go to **www.usborne-quicklinks.com** for a link to the **BBC Web site** to see the effects of an increasing human population.

• Go to **www.usborne-quicklinks.com** for a link to the **6 billion Human Beings Web site** for an excellent look at population growth and control.

• Go to **www.usborne-quicklinks.com** for a link to the **Biodiversity and Conservation Web site** to investigate the problem of rapid population growth.

• Go to **www.usborne-quicklinks.com** for a link to the **Population Reference Bureau Web site** to for population info.

• Go to **www.usborne-quicklinks.com** for a link to the **PopNet Web site**, an in-depth global population resource.

EARTH'S RESOURCES

Beneath the Earth's surface are many resources which are used by people all over the world. Some of these are precious stones, which can be sold or traded; others are metals, which are used for building and other purposes. Almost all the fuel currently used also comes from within the Earth.

This drink can contains aluminum, one of several metals that can be melted down and reused.

FOSSIL FUELS

Oil, coal and gas are known as **fossil fuels**. They are formed from the remains of plants and animals which have built up in rock for millions of years. The chemical energy trapped in these organisms is released when fossil fuels are burned.

Coal is formed from the remains of ancient plants.

People need fuel for cooking, heating, lighting, running motor vehicles, generating electricity, and many other things. But demand is great and supplies are limited, so all of the Earth's oil and gas may be used up within a few decades. This means that people need to find other fuel sources to meet their needs.

RENEWABLE ENERGY

Sources of energy which will not run out are described as **renewable**. These include the Sun's rays, which are captured by solar panels*; the wind, which turns wind turbines*; and moving water, used in hydroelectric power stations. **Geothermal energy** (heat energy from underground rocks) is used in volcanic areas. **Biogas**, which is given out by rotting waste, can also be burned to produce heat.

However, only 5% of the Earth's energy currently comes from renewable sources. This is mainly because they are often less reliable or less efficient than fossil fuels. For instance, many rely on certain climatic conditions, such as strong winds or constant, bright sunshine, which are not always available in some areas.

NUCLEAR POWER

Nuclear energy is produced from radioactive substances, such as uranium, when their tiny particles, called atoms, are broken apart. Many people believe it could be the most convenient energy source for the future, but it creates dangerous radioactive waste, which is difficult to dispose of safely.

Waste from nuclear power plants may remain dangerous for thousands of years. Radioactive material is labeled with a warning symbol.

These rows of huge, reflective solar panels capture the Sun's rays and use the energy to generate electricity.

Solar power provides a clean, safe form of energy.

MINERALS

For centuries, people have dug rocks out of the Earth because of the useful **minerals** they contain. Minerals are usually made up of a mixture of elements, for instance carbon, silicon and metals such as iron.

Gemstones, such as these garnets, are minerals which are mined for their beauty. They are usually cut and polished before being sold.

Rocks which contain a high level of minerals, particularly metals, are called **ores**. Metal ores taken from the Earth have to be processed to extract the pure metal. There are various ways of doing this, including smelting*, which involves heat, and electrolysis, which uses electricity.

Iron is extracted from an ore called **hematite**.

MINING

Rocks which contain useful minerals are **mined**, or taken from the ground. The mining technique used depends on the depth, value and amount of the ore. If it is found in large amounts underground, tunnels are dug beneath the Earth's surface to reach it. Ore near the surface can be dug out from an open pit.

Here, coal is being extracted from a mine at the surface of the ground. This is called an **open cast** mine.

Although people rely heavily on mining to supply many substances that they need, it can be bad for the environment. Mining for a single ton of ore may produce thousands of tons of waste rock, which may be spread over a wide area. Plant and animal life in the areas around a mine may be badly affected.

MANAGING RESOURCES

People have always depended on metals, fuels and the Earth's other natural resources. But mining and extracting different fuels and ores is an expensive and difficult process. Some substances, such as oil, are also becoming harder to find, as the best sources have already been used up.

At some time in the future, there will no longer be enough non-renewable resources to meet everyone's needs. Reusing and recycling materials, and using renewable fuel sources wherever possible, are the best ways to make the Earth's existing resources last as long as possible.

See for yourself

There are many materials which can be recycled. These include paper, glass, aluminum cans and steel. You could find out if there are any recycling centers near where you live. Your school might also organize recycling activities.

You can help save energy by remembering to switch off lights when leaving a room, or by asking your parents to use energy-efficient light bulbs, like this one.

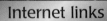

Internet links

- Go to **www.usborne-quicklinks.com** for a link to the **Environmental Index Web site** to learn about recycling, waste management and environmental issues.

- Go to **www.usborne-quicklinks.com** for a link to the **Coal Mine Homepage**, where you can take a virtual interactive tour of a coal mine to compare mining in the 1930s with the present day.

- Go to **www.usborne-quicklinks.com** for links to the **Atomic Alchemy: Nuclear Processes** and **Discovery Web sites** for information about many different aspects of nuclear energy.

FACTS AND LISTS

These pages contain lists of some amazing facts about Earth, the planets, and space exploration. They are as accurate as possible, but there are different ways of measuring things, so you may find slightly different figures elsewhere.

THE CONTINENTS

Name	Area (km²)
Asia	43,608,000
Africa	30,335,000
North America	24,300,000
South America	17,611,000
Antarctica	13,340,000
Europe	10,498,000
Australasia	8,923,000

OCEANS AND SEAS

The largest ocean, the Pacific, is also the deepest. At one point in an area called the Mariana Trench, it is 11,022m deep.

Name	Area (km²)
Pacific Ocean	166,241,000
Atlantic Ocean	82,217,000
Indian Ocean	73,600,000
Southern Ocean	35,000,000
Arctic Ocean	12,257,000
Mediterranean Sea	2,505,000
South China Sea	2,318,000
Caribbean Sea	1,943,000
Bering Sea	2,269,000
Gulf of Mexico	1,544,000

LARGEST ISLANDS

Name(s)	Area (km²)
Greenland (Kalaallit Nunaat)	2,175,600
New Guinea	789,950
Borneo	751,100
Madagascar	586,376
Baffin Island, Canada	507,454
Sumatra, Indonesia	424,760
Honshu, Japan	227,920
Great Britain	218,896
Victoria Island, Canada	217,290
Ellesmere Island, Canada	196,236

GREATEST LAKES

The deepest lake, at 1,637m, is Lake Baykal in Russia. It also contains the most fresh water.

Name(s)	Location	Area (km²)
Caspian Sea	Europe/Asia	424,200
Lake Superior	USA/Canada	82,414
Lake Victoria	Tanzania/Uganda	69,215
Lake Huron	USA/Canada	59,596
Lake Michigan	USA	58,016
Aral Sea	Kazakhstan/Uzbekistan	40,500
Lake Tanganyika	Tanzania/Congo	32,764
Lake Baykal	Russia	31,500
Great Bear Lake	Canada	31,328
Lake Nyasa (Malawi)	Mozambique/Tanzania	29,928

LONGEST RIVERS

Name(s)	Location	Length (km)
Nile (Bahr-el-Nil)	North-east Africa	6,671
Amazon (Amazonas)	South America	6,440
Chang Jiang (Yangtze-Kiang)	China	6,276
Mississippi-Missouri-Red Rock	USA	6,019
Ob'-Irtysh	Asia	5,411
Yenisei-Angara	Russia	4,989
Huang Ho (Yellow River)	China	4,830
Amur-Shilka-Onon	East Asia	4,416
Lena	Russia	4,400
Congo (Zaïre; Lualaba)	Central Africa	4,380

HIGHEST MOUNTAINS

Some lists include Lhotse in fourth position at 8,501m, but we have regarded it as a peak of Everest rather than a separate mountain.

Name(s)	Location	Height (m)
Everest	Nepal/Tibet border	8,848
K2 (Chogori)	Pakistan/China border	8,611
Kanchenjunga	Nepal/Sikkim border	8,598
Makalu	Nepal/Tibet border	8,470
Cho Oyu	Nepal/Tibet border	8,201
Dhaulagiri	Nepal	8,172
Manaslu	Nepal	8,163
Nanga Parbat	Pakistan	8,126
Annapurna	Nepal	8,078
Gasherbrum	Pakistan/China border	8,068

PLANETARY FACTS AND FIGURES

Name of planet	Diameter of planet	Average distance from Sun	Time to orbit Sun	Time to rotate	Number of satellites
Mercury	4,880km	58 million km	88 days	58.7 days	0
Venus	12,103km	108 million km	224.7 days	243 days	0
Earth	12,756km	149.6 million km	365.3 days	23.9 hours	1
Mars	6,794km	228 million km	687 days	24.6 hours	2
Jupiter	142,984km	778 million km	11.9 years	9.8 hours	At least 28
Saturn	120,536km	1,429 million km	29.5 years	10.2 hours	At least 24
Uranus	51,118km	2,870 million km	84 years	17.9 hours	21
Neptune	49,532km	4,504 million km	165 years	19.2 hours	8
Pluto	2,274km	5,913 million km	248 years	6.4 days	1

SPACE MISSIONS

1957 Sputnik 1, the first artificial satellite was launched into space on October 4 by the Soviet Union. On November 3, Sputnik 2 was launched into space, carrying a dog named Laika.

1959 The first space probes, Luna 1, Luna 2 and Luna 3, were sent to the Moon by the Soviet Union.

1961 Soviet cosmonaut Yuri Gagarin became the first person to travel into space. The flight lasted about 90 minutes.

1965 US astronomers detected weak signals, like radio noise, from space. Many people think that these prove the Big Bang theory.

1965 US space probe Mariner 4 took the first photos of Mars.

1966 Soviet space probe Luna 9 landed on the Moon, returning the first photos from its surface.

1967 Soviet Venera 4 became the first space probe to reach Venus. One day later, US probe Mariner 5 also reached Venus.

1968 The USA launched Apollo 8, the first manned space flight around the Moon.

1969 On July 20, the US Apollo 11 mission landed the first men on the Moon. They were Edwin "Buzz" Aldrin and Neil Armstrong, who was the first man to walk on the Moon. Another manned mission, Apollo 12, reached the Moon on November 14.

1970 US Apollo 13 Moon mission was cancelled when an explosion destroyed the main module's power system.

1971 Manned US Apollo 14 and Apollo 15 missions landed on the Moon's surface.

1971 The Russians launched the first space station, Salyut 1.

1971 US Mariner 9 space probe returned the first close-up images of Mars.

1972 Manned US Apollo 16 and Apollo 17 missions landed on the Moon's surface.

1973 The USA launched Skylab, the first US space station.

1973 US Pioneer 10 probe returned the first close-up pictures of Jupiter.

1974 US Mariner 10 space probe returned the first photos of cloud-tops around Venus. It then went on to Mercury, sending back over 10,000 pictures of the planet.

1975 Soviet space probes Venera 9 and Venera 10 took the first photos of Venus's surface.

1976 US space probes Viking 1 and Viking 2 landed on Mars. They took many photos and studied samples of Martian soil.

1979 US space probes Voyager 1 and Voyager 2 flew by Jupiter, sending back detailed pictures.

1980 US space probe Voyager 2 flew past Saturn, sending back detailed pictures.

1981 USA launched STS1, the first Space Shuttle flight.

1986 US probe Voyager 2 flew past Uranus, sending back detailed images.

1986 Soviet space station Mir was launched.

1986 US Space Shuttle Challenger exploded, killing seven astronauts.

1989 US space probe Voyager 2 flew by Neptune, sending back detailed pictures.

1991 The Hubble Space Telescope was launched from the USA. It was found to have a fault which prevented it sending back clear images.

1993 Spacewalking astronauts repaired the Hubble Space Telescope.

1993 US Galileo probe took the first close-up pictures of an asteroid, Gaspra.

1996 US NEAR (Near Earth Asteroid Rendezvous) spacecraft was launched to study near-Earth asteroids.

1996 US Mars Global Surveyor was launched to study Mars while in orbit around the planet.

1997 US Mars Pathfinder reached Mars, releasing a small rover vehicle named Sojourner onto the surface. It gathered detailed information about Martian soil, rocks and weather.

1998 Construction of the International Space Station began.

2001 The Mir space station became the largest man-made object to be brought back to Earth. It broke up on re-entry into the atmosphere, before landing in the Pacific Ocean.

MEASURING EARTHQUAKES

The energy of the underground shock waves that cause earthquakes is measured with a device called a **seismometer**. This uses the **Richter scale**. The impact of an earthquake above ground, rated by its effects, is often measured on the **Mercalli scale**.

Mercalli	Effects	Richter
1	Detectable only by seismometers.	0-2.9
2	Only a few people on upper floors notice.	3-3.4
3	Like a heavy truck passing by. Hanging lights may swing.	3.5-4
4	Windows and dishes rattle. Like a heavy truck crashing into building.	4.1-4.4
5	Almost everyone notices. Sleepers wake up. Small objects move and drinks spill.	4.5-4.8
6	Many people frightened and run outdoors. Heavy furniture moves. Pictures fall off walls.	4.9-5.4
7	Walls crack. Tiles and bricks fall from buildings. Difficult to stand up.	5.5-6
8	Some weaker buildings collapse. Mass panic may break out.	6.1-6.5
9	Well-built houses collapse. Underground pipes damaged. Cracks open in ground.	6.6-7
10	Landslides. Rivers overflow. Many stone buildings collapse.	7.1-7.3
11	Most buildings destroyed. Large cracks in ground.	7.4-8.1
12	Ground moves in waves. Total destruction.	8.2+

THE BEAUFORT SCALE

The **Beaufort Scale** was developed in 1805 by Sir Francis Beaufort, a British Navy Commander, to estimate wind speed at sea. In the 1920s it was extended to include precise wind speeds and adapted for use on land. While it is now rarely used by **meteorologists** (weather scientists), it is still a popular means of calculating wind speed without using instruments.

Beaufort number	Miles per hour	Wind description
0	Less than 1	Calm
1	1-3	Light air movement
2	4-7	Slight breeze
3	8-12	Gentle breeze
4	13-18	Moderate breeze
5	19-24	Fresh breeze
6	25-31	Strong breeze
7	32-38	Moderate gale (or high wind)
8	39-46	Gale
9	47-54	Strong gale
10	55-63	Storm
11*	64-73	Violent storm
12*	74 or more	Hurricane

* Storms this strong usually only happen at sea.

TEST YOURSELF

1. At the center of the Solar System lies:
A. a moon
B. the Sun
C. the Earth   *(Page 17)*

2. Planet Earth makes a complete orbit around the Sun once every:
A. day
B. month
C. year   *(Page 17)*

3. The four inner planets, which are all rocky and fairly small, are:
A. Earth, Venus, Mercury, Mars
B. Pluto, Neptune, Saturn, Uranus
C. Venus, Mars, Saturn, Neptune
                    (Page 18)

4. The Moon orbits the Earth:
A. once every week
B. once every 28 days
C. once every year   *(Page 21)*

5. The Moon shines at night because:
A. it is made of pale, shiny rock
B. it reflects light from the Sun
C. it gives out its own light   *(Page 21)*

6. Man-made devices that orbit the Earth, gathering information, are called:
A. satellites
B. observatories
C. refractors   *(Page 29)*

7. Spreading ridges are found at plate boundaries which are:
A. constructive
B. destructive
C. sedimentary   *(Page 36)*

8. High fold mountain ranges are formed when two continental plates:
A. slide past each other
B. move apart
C. push together   *(Page 35)*

9. When hot, molten rocks cool and harden, the rock formed is called:
A. continental
B. metamorphic
C. igneous   *(Page 35)*

10. The point directly above an earthquake's focus is its:
A. seismic wave
B. epicenter
C. eruption   *(Page 36)*

11. Magma in volcanoes which form above subduction zones has come from:
A. a spreading ridge
B. the descending plate
C. a hot spot   *(Page 37)*

12. Aa sudden increase in the number of animals with hard parts happened:
A. in the Carboniferous Period
B. in the Cambrian Period
C. in the Permian Period   *(Page 41)*

13. The world's largest ocean is the:
A. Pacific Ocean
B. Atlantic Ocean
C. Southern Ocean   *(Page 42)*

14. The ocean tides are caused mainly by the pull of gravity on the water by:
A. the Moon
B. the Sun
C. the Solar System   *(Page 42)*

15. In the Far East, hurricanes are called:
A. depressions
B. typhoons
C. cyclones   *(Page 43)*

16. The source of a river is where it:
A. starts
B. ends
C. meanders   *(Page 44)*

17. Wide loops in the middle and lower reaches of a river are called:
A. sediments
B. deltas
C. meanders   *(Page 44)*

18. A river's speed normally increases as it moves from the upper stage to the lower stage. This is mainly because:
A. the river's width increases
B. a flood plain develops
C. the bed becomes smoother so there is less friction to slow down the water   *(Page 44)*

19. All of the material carried by a river is called its:
A. flood plain
B. load
C. gradient   *(Page 45)*

20. Tiny water droplets form clouds when water vapor in the air:
A. disintegrates
B. evaporates
C. condenses   *(Page 47)*

21. In July the northern hemisphere has its summer because:
A. there are fewer clouds in the sky
B. the Sun gives out more heat in July
C. the northern hemisphere is tilted toward the Sun   *(Page 47)*

22. In mountainous districts the climate changes mainly with
A. attitude
B. altitude
C. latitude   *(Page 49)*

23. A mild, wet coastal climate is also known as a:
A. Marine climate
B. Meridian climate
C. Maritime climate   *(Page 49)*

24. Over the next 100 years the world's population is expected to:
A. level off
B. decrease
C. continue increasing   *(Page 50)*

25. The general movement of people from the countryside to cities is called:
A. commuting
B. urban migration
C. rural migration   *(Page 50)*

26. For many people the main reason they move into cities is:
A. to find a job
B. to farm the land
C. to build a home   *(Page 50)*

27. All the materials needed by humans and provided by the Earth are:
A. resources
B. food
C. fuel   *(Page 52)*

28. Oil and coal are examples of:
A. fossil fuels
B. nuclear fuels
C. renewable fuels   *(Page 52)*

29. Energy sources which do not rely on fossil fuels are described as:
A. temporary
B. renewable
C. non-renewable   *(Page 52)*

30. One good way of using the Earth's resources so they last longer is:
A. extracting
B. mining
C. recycling   *(Page 53)*

Answers

1.B 2.C 3.A 4.B 5.B 6.A 7.A 8.C 9.C 10.B 11.B 12.B 13.A 14.A 15.B 16.A 17.C 18.C 19.B 20.C 21.C 22.B 23.C 24.C 25.B 26.A 27.A 28.A 29.B 30.C

57

A-Z OF SCIENTIFIC TERMS

Absolute magnitude The actual brightness of a star in space.
abyssal zone The cold, dark, level of the ocean found from 4,375 yards downward.
altitude Height above sea level.
amphibian A type of cold-blooded, soft-skinned animal, which lives both on land and in water, for example a frog.
apparent magnitude A star's brightness seen from the Earth.
arthropod A type of creature with a segmented body, jointed legs and a hard exoskeleton, for example a lobster.
aspect The compass direction a mountainside faces.
asterisms Smaller patterns of stars within a constellation.
asteroids Large lumps of rock and metal, most of which orbit the Sun in a region called the **Asteroid Belt** between Mars and Jupiter.
asthenosphere A weak, partly molten layer in the Earth's mantle, upon which the whole lithosphere moves.
astrophysics The science of the physical and chemical aspects of heavenly bodies.
atmosphere 1. The protective layer of air around the Earth that enables plants and animals to live. 2. A layer of gases around any planet.
atmospheric pressure The force of the air pressing down on the Earth's surface, measured in **millibars** (**mb**). At sea level, it is stated as one atmosphere (1 atm), also known as **standard pressure**, and equal to 1,013 mb.
aurora A display of lights in the sky caused by particles from the solar wind trapped in the Earth's atmosphere near the poles. The display is called the **Aurora Borealis** (or northern lights) in the north and the **Aurora Australis** (or southern lights) in the south.

Barred spiral galaxy A spiral galaxy with a central bar of stars and an arm at each end.
Beaufort scale A scale of measurement of wind speed, based on observation rather than calculation with instruments.
Big Bang theory The idea that time and all the matter in the universe came into being with a massive explosion known as the Big Bang.
Big Crunch theory The idea that gravity will slow down the expansion of the universe, pulling everything back until all the galaxies crash together.
binary star Two stars orbiting each other.

biogases Burnable gases, produced by rotting organic matter, used as fuel.
black hole An area of such strong gravitational pull that no matter or energy can escape from it, thought to form after the largest supernovas.

Caldera A very large crater formed when the upper part of a volcano either blows off or collapses into the magma chamber below.
carbonaceous (**C-type**) A term describing asteroids that contain carbon. They are the most common.
cataclysmic variable A binary star in which the two stars are close enough for one to pull material away from the other. When this happens, there is a sudden increase in brightness.
CFCs (**chlorofluorocarbons**) Organic compounds of carbon, fluorine and chlorine, that are believed to damage the atmosphere.
cirrus A high, wispy type of cloud.
climate A typical pattern of weather conditions over a long period of time.
climatic region A large area of the Earth in which the climate is generally the same.
coastal climate (or **maritime climate**) A mild, wet climate.
coma The cloud of gas and dust streaming out as a tail from a melting comet's nucleus.
comet A huge chunk of frozen gas and dirt that travels around the Sun in a wide, oval orbit which takes it far away for long periods of time.
constellation One of 88 recognizable patterns of stars in the night sky.
constructive boundary A tectonic plate boundary where new lithosphere is formed.
continent Any of the large landmasses into which the Earth is divided. Their central regions have hot summers and cold winters, with little influence from the air currents moving between the sea and the land at the coasts.
continental drift The slow movement of the continents, caused by the gradual shifting of the Earth's tectonic plates.
convection The way heat energy in liquids or gases is transferred. The part of a fluid nearest the heat source expands, becoming less dense, and rises; the denser, cooler part sinks.
convection current A movement of a liquid or gas caused by convection.
convective zone The part of the Sun between the radiative zone and the photosphere.
core The central part of an object, such as the Earth or the Sun.

Coriolis effect The deflection of winds from their direct paths between pressure belts, caused by the Earth's rotation.
corona A low-density layer of gas around the Sun, visible during a total solar eclipse.
crust The thin layer of solid rock that covers the Earth. Below it is the mantle.
C-type See *carbonaceous*.
cumulus A fluffy, white type of cloud which appears high up in warm, sunny weather.

Deep time See *geological time*.
delta A flat area of land, broken by many small channels, built up of material deposited by a river as it flows into a sea.
desert A climate that is very dry, with under 9.8 inches of rainfall per year.
destructive boundary (or **subduction zone**) A plate boundary where an oceanic plate melts partially as it moves beneath a continental plate, forming a trench on the surface.
dwarf star A star smaller than the Sun.
dyke A sheet of igneous rock formed from magma squeezed into existing rocks, cutting across them.

Earthquake A sudden movement of rock in the Earth's crust which releases built-up pressure. Shock waves called seismic waves spread out and may cause great damage.
eclipse The total or partial disappearance of a heavenly body when another one moves between it and the viewer.
eclipsing variable A binary star which varies in brightness as one star eclipses the other.
electromagnetic radiation Energy which travels in waves, such as light.
elliptical galaxy A galaxy, round or oval in shape, that contains many old, red stars.
epicenter The point on the Earth's surface directly above the focus of an earthquake.
Equator An imaginary line which runs around the middle of the Earth, dividing it into the northern and southern hemispheres.
equatorial A climate which is always hot and wet. Rainforests are found in equatorial regions.
Eras The four main divisions of geological time: Precambrian: 4,600-545 million years ago (mya); Paleozoic: 545-250 mya; Mesozoic: 250-65 mya; Cenozoic: 65 mya to the present day (numbers are approximate).

erosion The gradual wearing down of rock by wind, water or ice.

exosphere The outermost layer of the atmosphere, which merges into space.

Facula A cloud of glowing gases that often surrounds a sunspot.

faults Cracks in the Earth's surface rock, caused by plate movement.

fertigation Irrigation using water with added fertilizers.

flood plain The wide, flat floor of a river valley, that is covered with water when the river floods.

focus The point, usually deep underground, where the rock first gives way in an earthquake.

fold mountains Mountain ranges formed where plates push together.

fossil fuel A fuel such as coal, oil or natural gas, that is formed from the fossilized remains of plants or animals.

Galaxy A vast collection of stars, held together by gravitational attraction.

geological time (or **deep time**) A scale of millions of years used by geologists to measure the Earth's history.

geology The science of the Earth's origin and structure, and its rocks and minerals.

geostationary orbit The orbit of a satellite moving at the rate the Earth spins, so that it remains fixed over the same point.

geothermal energy Heat energy from underground rocks, used in some places to generate electricity by heating water to steam, which turns turbines.

giant star A star larger than the Sun.

glacier A huge sheet or ribbon of ice that moves slowly over the land.

global warming A rise in average temperatures around the world which scientists believe to be caused by the greenhouse effect.

globular cluster A densely packed, spherical collection of up to a million stars, moving at the same speed and in the same direction.

Great Red Spot A vast storm that rages constantly in Jupiter's atmosphere.

greenhouse effect The trapping of heat by carbon dioxide and other gases in the Earth's atmosphere.

Heavenly body Any naturally occurring object in space.

hot spot A small area on the Earth's surface where there is a great deal of volcanic activity. It lies above a concentration of particularly hot, rising magma, called **plumes**.

humidity The amount of water in the air.

hurricane See *tropical cyclone*.

hydroelectric power Power generated by turbines that are driven by falling water.

Ice ages Periods of the Earth's history when much of its surface was covered in glaciers.

igneous rock A type of rock formed when molten rock magma cools and becomes solid.

infrared radiation (**infrared rays**) Electromagnetic radiation given out by anything hot.

inner core The solid, innermost part of the Earth, which is about 776 miles thick and has a temperature of about 9,032°F.

irregular galaxy A galaxy with no definite shape or arrangement.

irrigation Making dry land suitable for agriculture by watering it.

Lava Magma that has erupted onto the Earth's surface.

light year The distance that light travels in one year – about 6 trillion miles.

lithosphere The outer, solid part of the Earth, made up of the crust and upper mantle.

Local Group The group of about 30 galaxies that includes the Milky Way.

low surface brightness galaxy A large galaxy of loosely packed stars that does not give off much light.

lunar eclipse The total or partial disappearance from view of the Moon due to the Earth's shadow.

Magma Molten underground rock which forms a small part of the mantle.

magma chamber An area where magma gathers beneath a volcano.

magnitude (**mag.**) The measurement of star brightness.

mantle The mostly solid part of the Earth that lies between the crust and the core.

maritime climate See *coastal climate*.

mass extinctions Five points in Earth's ancient past when huge numbers of living things died out in a very short time.

meander A wide loop in the course of a river channel.

Mercalli scale A scale of measurement of the intensity of earthquakes, based on the damage they inflict.

mesosphere A layer in the middle atmosphere containing no clouds or ozone.

metallic (**M-type**) A term describing asteroids composed of metals. They may be the exposed metal cores of originally much larger objects.

metamorphic rock The type of rock formed when another rock is changed by intense heat, pressure or both.

meteor (or **shooting star**) A meteoroid that is starting to burn up as it enters the atmosphere.

meteorite The remains of a meteor that has survived its journey through the atmosphere and landed on Earth.

meteoroid A small piece of space debris.

meteorology The science of weather and climate.

meteor shower A short spectacular display of meteors caused by the Earth crossing a comet's path.

microclimate A climate affecting just a small, local area.

Milky Way The galaxy in which our Solar System lies.

minerals The naturally occurring single or combined elements of which rocks are made.

moon A natural satellite orbiting a planet or asteroid.

M-type See *metallic*.

Neap tides The lowest tides, which occur at every half moon, when the Sun and Moon are at right angles to each other in relation to Earth.

nebula A huge cloud of dust and gas inside which stars form.

neutron star A small, spinning, exceptionally dense star that is left after a supernova.

northern lights See *aurora*.

nova A type of cataclysmic variable which flares suddenly for a number of days or years, then fades back to its original brightness.

nuclear energy The energy held in the nucleus of an atom.

nuclear fusion A reaction in which the nuclei of atoms join, or fuse, together, forming new atoms and releasing huge amounts of energy.

nucleus 1. The main body of a comet, made up of frozen gases, ice, rock and grit. 2. The core of an atom, made up of even smaller particles called protons and (except hydrogen) neutrons.

Observatory A building which houses a large telescope for studying stars.

open cluster A collection of between a few dozen and a thousand loosely scattered stars, moving in the same direction at the same speed.

orbit 1. To circle around an object. 2. The path taken when orbiting.

ore A mineral compound from which a metal can be extracted.

Oscillating Universe theory The idea that the universe expands and shrinks, in a repeating cycle of Big Bangs and Big Crunches.

outer core The molten outer layer of the Earth's core, which is about 1,375 miles thick.

outgassing The process by which gases poured out of volcanoes, forming the Earth's early atmosphere.

ozone layer The protective layer of ozone gas in the stratosphere, which absorbs harmful ultraviolet radiation from the Sun.

Pangaea A single giant landmass that began to split up about 225 million years ago, leading to the formation of the present-day continents.

periods Subdivisions of geological Eras, each measuring several million years.

permeable A term describing things which have holes, or pores, that let in water.

phases The different shapes made by the sunlit portion of the Moon's near side as it orbits the Earth. For example, a crescent.

photosphere The surface of the Sun, made up of churning gases.

phytoplankton Microscopic plants found near the surface of seas and oceans.

planet One of the nine spherical bodies orbiting the Sun, or any other similar bodies orbiting other stars.

plate boundaries The areas where the edges of the Earth's tectonic plates meet.

plates Sections of the Earth's lithosphere, which move around on the asthenosphere and fit together like the pieces of a jigsaw puzzle.

plate tectonics The study of the movement of the Earth's tectonic plates.

polar climate A harsh climate with extremely low temperatures and little precipitation or plant life.

precipitation Rain, sleet, snow or hail.

prevailing winds The most frequent direction of winds in an area.

primary The brighter star in a binary star (pair of stars).

prominence A huge loop of flaming gas that leaps off the Sun's surface.

pulsar A neutron star that sends out beams of radiation which swing around as it spins.

pulsating variable A variable star that changes in brilliance as it changes in size and temperature.

Radiative zone The part of the Sun that surrounds its core.

red giant The swollen red form taken by a giant star as it dies.

red supergiant The swollen red form taken by a supergiant star as it dies.

renewable energy resources Sources of energy such as the Sun, wind or water, that can be used to generate power without being used up.

Richter scale The scale of measurement of the size and strength of earthquakes, based on seismometer readings.

ridge See *spreading ridge*.

rift valley The type of valley formed when the area of rock between two faults collapses as the land is forced in opposite directions.

Satellites Any objects orbiting a star, planet or asteroid, including the man-made devices orbiting the Earth that are used to gather data or receive and transmit radio signals.

secondary The dimmer star in a binary star (pair of stars).

sediment Material rich in minerals, which is laid down over time by rivers and glaciers, and eventually squashed into rock.

sedimentary rock The type of rock formed when mineral particles are deposited, buried and squashed into layers.

seismic waves The shock waves that travel outward from the focus of an earthquake.

seismologist A scientist who studies earthquakes.

seismometer A device that measures the energy of seismic waves.

shooting star See *meteor*.

silicaceous (S-type) A term describing asteroids that contain metal silicates (compounds of metals, silicon and oxygen). They are bright and shiny.

Slowing Down theory The idea that the universe could expand continuously and gradually fade away.

soil erosion The wearing away of topsoil by wind or rain.

solar eclipse The total or partial disappearance from view of the Sun due to the Moon coming between it and the Earth.

solar energy See *solar radiation*.

solar flare A brief but violent explosion from the Sun's surface.

solar prominence See *prominence*.

solar radiation (or **solar energy**) Electromagnetic radiation emitted by the Sun, made up of ultraviolet rays, visible light and infrared rays.

Solar System Our Sun, together with all the planets and other objects orbiting it.

solar wind A constant stream of invisible particles blown out into space from the Sun.

southern lights See *aurora*.

space probes Unmanned spacecraft sent to explore the Solar System and beyond.

space station A large satellite orbiting the Earth, where astronauts can live and perform scientific research over fairly long periods.

spectral type The class of a star.

spiral galaxy A galaxy with a bright middle and two or more curved arms of stars.

spreading ridge A boundary where two tectonic plates are moving away from each other. Magma wells up to fill the gap, forming a large, long ridge on the ocean floor.

spring tides The highest tides, which occur at the full and new moon.

standard pressure See *atmospheric pressure*.

star A ball of tremendously hot gas which produces heat and light from nuclear reactions in its core.

strata Layers of sedimentary rock.

stratosphere A layer in the middle atmosphere containing the ozone layer.

stratus A type of cloud that forms low in the sky in flat, gray layers.

S-type See *silicaceous*.

subduction zone See *destructive boundary*.

sunless zone The level of the ocean between 1,095 yards and 4,375 yards in depth, where no sunlight reaches.

sunlit zone The top 220 yards of the ocean, home to many animals and all sea plants.

sunspot A small, dark, slightly cooler patch on the Sun.

supergiant star The largest star type.

supernova A colossal explosion that occurs when a giant star dies.

supervolcano A huge, powerful volcano, the eruption of which would cause massive environmental damage.

Temperate climate A climate with rainfall all year and temperatures that vary with the seasons.

thermosphere An extremely hot layer of the upper atmosphere.

trench A long, deep, steep-sided trough formed at a destructive boundary between two plates.

tributary A river or stream that flows into a larger one.

tropical climate A warm climate with two seasons: dry and wet.

tropical cyclone (or **hurricane** or **typhoon**) A fierce storm caused by warm ocean currents.

troposphere The lowest layer of the atmosphere, containing 80% of its gases and all of its weather.

tundra A region with harsh winds and low winter temperatures. Its underground soil is always frozen, so it has no trees.

twilight zone The level of the ocean between 220 yards and 1,095 yards in depth, where very little sunlight reaches.

typhoon See *tropical cyclone*.

Ultraviolet radiation (ultraviolet rays) Electromagnetic radiation with more energy than visible light. It can cause damage if too much is absorbed.

urban migration The movement of people from country to city areas in search of work.

Variable star A star that changes gradually in brilliance.

vent The main pipe up the middle of a volcano.

volcanic bomb A lump of lava blasted into the air during a volcanic eruption.

volcano An opening in the Earth's surface formed by magma bursting out (as lava), usually forming a conical moun

White dwarf The stage in the death of a giant star that comes after the red giant has lost its gas layers. It is small and extremely dense, and gradually cools and fades.

INDEX

You will find the main explanations of terms in the index on the pages shown in bold type. It may be useful to look at the other pages for further information.

ACKNOWLEDGEMENTS

PHOTO CREDITS
(t = top, m = middle, b = bottom, l = left, r = right)

Corbis: **6-7** Julia Waterlow, Eye Ubiquitous; **20** (mr) NASA/Roger Ressmeyer; **28-29** (b) Roger Ressmeyer; **38-39** (main) Galen Rowell; **46-47** (t) L. Clarke; **50-51** (main) Hans Georg Roth; **52-53** (b) Roger Ressmeyer.
Digital Imagery© Copyright 2001 PhotoDisc, Inc: **2-3**; **4-5**.
© **Digital Vision**: **cover**; **1**; **8** (bl); **10** (tr), (br); **12** (l); **15** (mr); **16** (t), (b); **17** (t); **18** (tr); **19** (tm); **20** (tr), (ml), (m), (b); **21** (t); **24-25** (t); **27** (l); **29** (tr); **30** (br); **30-31**; **31** (mr), (bl); **32** (tr); **33** (ml); **34-35**; **36-37**; **39** (t), (m), (ml); **41** (mr); **42** (tr);**42-43**; **44-45**; **46** (b); **47** (l), (m); **48** (m), (bm); **48-49** (b); **50** (tr), (ml); **51** (m); **53** (m); **54-55**.
NASA: **15** (tl), (bl); **18-19** (b); **19** (mr); **24** (bl), (br); **25** (bl); **29** (m); **32** (b).
Stuart Atkinson 26 (tr)

ILLUSTRATORS
Simone Abel, Sophie Allington, Rex Archer, Paul Bambrick, Jeremy Banks, Andrew Beckett, Joyce Bee, Stephen Bennett, Roland Berry, Gary Bines, Isabel Bowring, Trevor Boyer, John Brettoner, Peter Bull, Hilary Burn, Andy Burton, Terry Callcut, Kuo Kang Chen, Stephen Conlin, Sydney Cornfield, Dan Courtney, Steve Cross, Gordon Davies, Peter Dennis, Richard Draper, Brin Edwards, Sandra Fernandez, Denise Finney, John Francis, Mark Franklin, Nigel Frey, Giacinto Gaudenzi, Peter Geissler, Nick Gibbard, William Giles, David Goldston, Peter Goodwin, Jeremy Gower, Teri Gower, Terry Hadler, Bob Hersey, Nicholas Hewetson, Christine Howes, Inklink Firenze, Ian Jackson, Karen Johnson, Richard Johnson, Elaine Keenan, Aziz Khan, Stephen Kirk, Richard Lewington, Brian Lewis, Jason Lewis, Steve Lings, Rachel Lockwood, Kevin Lyles, Chris Lyon, Kevin Maddison, Janos Marffy, Andy Martin, Josephine Martin, Peter Massey, Rob McCaig, Joseph McEwan, David McGrail, Malcolm McGregor, Christina McInerney, Caroline McLean, Dee McLean, Annabel Milne, Sean Milne, Robert Morton, Louise Nevet, Martin Newton, Louise Nixon, Steve Page, Justine Peek, Mick Posen, Russell Punter, Barry Raynor, Mark Roberts, Andrew Robinson, Michael Roffe, Michelle Ross, Michael Saunders, John Scorey, John Shackell, Chris Shields, David Slinn, Guy Smith, Peter Stebbing, Robert Walster, Craig Warwick, Ross Watton, Phil Weare, Hans Wiborg-Jenssen, Sean Wilkinson, Ann Winterbottom, Gerald Wood, David Wright.

Every effort has been made to trace the copyright holders of the material in this book. If any rights have been omitted, the publishers offer to rectify this in any future edition, following notification.

American editor: Carrie A. Seay. With thanks to US expert Dr Janet Mercer.